Gerald F Cox

THE RADICAL PEASANT

GERALD F. COX

TRAFFORD

USA ▪ Canada ▪ UK ▪ Ireland

Note for Librarians: A cataloguing record for this book is available from Library and Archives Canada at www.collectionscanada.ca/amicus/index-e.html
ISBN 1-4120-9557-3

Printed in Victoria, BC, Canada. Printed on paper with minimum 30% recycled fibre. Trafford's print shop runs on "green energy" from solar, wind and other environmentally-friendly power sources.

TRAFFORD.
PUBLISHING™

Offices in Canada, USA, Ireland and UK

Book sales for North America and international:
Trafford Publishing, 6E–2333 Government St.,
Victoria, BC V8T 4P4 CANADA
phone 250 383 6864 (toll-free 1 888 232 4444)
fax 250 383 6804; email to orders@trafford.com
Book sales in Europe:
Trafford Publishing (UK) Limited, 9 Park End Street, 2nd Floor
Oxford, UK OX1 1HH UNITED KINGDOM
phone +44 (0)1865 722 113 (local rate 0845 230 9601)
facsimile +44 (0)1865 722 868; info.uk@trafford.com
Order online at:
trafford.com/06-1312

10 9 8 7 6 5 4

To John Ralph Duggan, lifetime friend and mentor.

Navarro, California

June, 2002

ACKNOWLEDGEMENTS

∽◦◦◯◦◦∽

During the course of gathering materials and information for this volume, I had the opportunity to interview many individuals who knew Charles Philipps intimately and who had experienced him in different settings. Each one represents a piece of the mosaic that this biography tries to create. I wish to acknowledge and thank each one of them for enriching the story of Charlie's life. In a real sense this is also your work besides mine. If there are other people whom I have inadvertently failed to mention, I am thankful for your input.

John Duggan to whom this book is dedicated, and who served five years as Charlie's assistant at St. Mary's Church, supplied many details of Charlie's character and the neighborhood of St. Mary's Parish.

Father Bill O'Donnell of St. Joseph The Worker Parish, Berkeley, California, who served as Charlie's chauffeur at Sunshine Camp, offered many comical and interesting events at the camp.

Father Don McDonnell, Charlie's successor as Catholic Rural Life Director, deserves a special recognition and thank you for collecting all of Charlie's papers and delivering them to the Archdiocese of San Francisco's Archives located at St.. Patrick's Seminary, Menlo Park, California.

The late Monsignor James B.. Flynn who lived at St. Mary's Rectory during his seminary days was appointed by Charlie as Head Counselors of Sunshine Camp.

Ms. Peggy Squires of Santa Rosa, a lifelong friend from Sebastopol days, provided a wealth of tales and descriptions of Philipps' activities in Sebastopol. Pete and Rose Sharp also contributed early stories.

REVEREND CHARLES PHILIPPS

1881-1958

" Here is my beloved servant whom I behold,

My chosen one in whom I delight. I have put my spirit upon him,

And he will bring justice to the nations."

Isiah 42:1-2

The late Sister Eileen Marie Cronin, SMJM described the role of the Sisters of the Holy Names at St. Mary's School and some humorous remembrances of Charlie's relationship with the sisters.

Sister Laurence Marie Revel, SMJM, formerly Alice Revel, prior to her entrance into the Holy Names Sisters, was a deep source of information on personalities and life at Sunshine Camp.

Sister Roseanne Curtis, SSS, a Sister of Social Service, described the activities and apostolate of the sisters in the St. Mary's community as well as historical information of her community.

Mr. Jeffery M. Burns, PhD, Archivist of the San Francisco Archdiocesan Archives at St. Patrick's Seminary, Menlo Park, California, allowed me full access to Charlie's papers and kept encouraging me to finish this biography.

Kenneth M. Schaffer, Jr., Librarian and Archivist at the Brethren Historical Library and Archives, Elgin, Illinois, for information of the Heifer Project.

The California State Offices of the California Grange, Sacramento, California, for access to their annual reports of the 1930's and 1940's.

Father Ron Burke who followed me at St. Mary's for providing me the litany of quotes from the Joe Pier days.

Bill Cane, another product of Charlie's "practical school of social service", allowed me to include his KING OF THE PEASANTS portrait.

Special thanks also must go to a number of West Oakland/St. Mary's people such as Rosemary Escobar, Bob Valva, Evelio Grillo, and Father Tony Valdivia for their recollection of Charlie, St. Mary's Parish, West Oakland, and the Mexican Community.

Also, I am sincerely grateful to my hosts in Alsace, France, Charles Philipps and Jean Marie Philipps for invaluable research of the Philipps' family of Stundwiller, Alsace, photographs, and family tales.

I cannot thank Ms. MeMe Riordan of San Francisco enough for accepting the "pro bono" role as the editor of this biography. She has corrected many pages of spelling, phrasing, and paragraphing. Her most valuable contribution was to make me delve into the character of my subject, Charles Philipps, especially his impact upon the development of my own social conscience. I am deeply indebted to her for any success of the book.

Finally I would like to thank all those friends who have assisted me with the expenses of this biography, especially the Y & H Soda Foundation, the Archdiocese of San Francisco Archives, and the Diocese of Oakland.

ABOUT THE AUTHOR

✿◦❍◦✿

$\mathscr{G}$erald F. Cox, 81, is a retired Catholic priest living in the rural Anderson Valley, Mendocino County, Northern California. As an active clergyman he served in the Archdiocese of San Francisco and the Diocese of Santa Rosa, California. His bi-lingual ability assisted his involvement with the Mexican communities and movements of the 60's.

He presently works with "at risk" Hispanic students and is active in developing affordable housing for local farm worker families. Together with his wife Kathleen Snyder, a former Peace Corps volunteer and present local high school Spanish teacher, they have two married daughters, Rebekah Rocha and Mary Anne Doble along with two grandsons, Gerald Cox Rocha and Cadence Doble.

❧❍❧

"This book should be required reading for any seminarian and for any Catholic disillusioned with today's Church. What Father Philipps accomplished is still present in the seminarians he formed, the priests he influenced, the children he touched, and the Church he loved. We desperately need more priests in the lineage and image of Pop Philipps. By reading this book, one meets a sterling priest, a magnificent leader, and a man of indisputable integrity and commitment."

Rev. Gerald D. Coleman, S.S.
St. Patrick's Seminary, Menlo Park, California

❧❍❧

"The Radical Peasant is a must read for anyone interested in Christian social justice and social activism. Its genre is an ingenious combination of memoir and biography. It is the fascinating story of a cultured but earthy immigrant priest devoted to anyone in need, especially children, the poor, and the farm workers of California. The author's reminiscences of his mentor and of the history surrounding his ministry are not only interesting but inspiring as well"

Raymond H. Potvin, Professor Emeritus
Department of Sociology
The Catholic University of America, Washington, D.C.

❧❍❧

"I am very happy that you are accused of Communism again. After all, such accusations must come your way now and then, or you would be failing in the main purpose of your life. I think we will meet a lot of Communists like you in Heaven."

Monsignor Luigi Ligutti,
Executive Secretary, National Catholic Rural Life Conference,
Des Moines, Iowa   January 20, 1949

CHAPTERS

FOREWORD

᠊ᢙᠥᢙ᠊

$\mathcal{O}$f the many stories we read about priests these days, few are more heartwarming, dramatic, socially relevant or humanly absorbing than this story about the Rev. Charles Philipps, who served actively and wisely for some forty-seven years as a priest, agrarian reformer, rural activist and consummate advocate to helping the people left behind in the urban ghettos and barrios where he was assigned. This story has great qualities: pathos, humor, conflict, inspiration and nostalgia.

A few years ago I was fortunate to acquire a near mint condition 1958 Bel Air Chevrolet covered with an abundance of heavy chrome, clear glass, shiny two tone paint and a body style that reflects durability and longevity. Whenever I drive into town, using rural country roads where I live, passing drivers inevitably smile, nod, or give me a thumbs up. When parked, strangers approach me with a smile and say something like, "what a nice ride," or mention previous ownership of such car in their family or a desire to own one. These are some of the same feelings this pleasing book evokes. Better still, it was not written by General Motors, but by a caring, knowledgeable and durable friend, Jerry Cox.

If it is true that the past can be a prologue to those who are willing to learn from it, then Jerry Cox makes a major contribution through this book, to our understanding of how one priest and others whose lives he touched can in Jerry's own words: "bring God to people by one's witness, and people to Him by living Christ's message through advocacy and fighting for the poor and oppressed."

No one knows this story better than Jerry Cox, who with his newly minted ordination as a young priest first encounters Rev. Philipps, then a recently retired Pastor at the end of his active priesthood at St. Mary's Church in West Oakland, California. Over the next five years of his residence there, Jerry had almost daily contact with Father Philipps who enjoyed having a close ear to talk to for hours on end. From there this story is told with gusto, great Irish humor and regard for a crusty old priest who were it not for the magnitude and importance of his advocacy for the poor could be regarded as somewhat of a character or odd ball. However humorous and circuitous his methods, Fr. Philipps was sensitive and appreciative of different cultures, was fluent in six languages, and a bon vivant with refined tastes in respect to food and drink. His patrician-like preferences did not appear to diminish his greater passion and commitment to helping those he dedicated to serve, the materially poor and marginalized.

Of the many stories included none is more awe inspiring than the accounts of the big issues Fr. Philipps confronted, including fights to end the "Bracero" program a contract system of hiring agricultural workers; campaigns to preserve provisions of the 160-acre Water Reclamation Act, and his tireless struggle against profit-centered corporate agriculture and the use of technological, financial and marketing integration to reduce the farm family to a sentimental memory.

Drawing from the depth of his own knowledge and experience as a seasoned advocate for the poor, Jerry Cox shares with us the many obstacles and hostility Fr. Philipps had to contend with, including the nuisance of having to deal with what Fr. Philipps termed, "damned ecclesiasticisms." With great affection and insight, Jerry Cox reveals how Fr. Philipps managed to get lots of things done, often in the face of stern and foreboding institutional authority.

Long before Cesar Chavez became known for surfacing the cause of farm workers, Fr. Philipps and the National Catholic Rural Life Conference were there advocating for public policy to improve working conditions, and wages for documented and undocumented workers in the fields. Undaunted, Fr. Philipps and a handful of priests from the San Francisco Archdiocese, loosely organized as "The Mission Band," courageously confronted the powerful interests of agribusiness, banks, power utilities, government, Associated Farmers and the silence and apathy of the Catholic Church hierarchy.

Within a short time the Band gained sufficient attention as to give the impression that somehow the Catholic Church had a larger strategy and commitment in place for dealing with the rapidly growing Hispanic presence in the United States -- a presence that ultimately overwhelmed the ability of the Church and other institutions to handle. Years before, Fr. Philipps anticipated this population surge of Hispanic communities in California and urged that the training of clergy include the teaching of Spanish. To emphasize that point, Fr. Philipps sent one of his priests, John Duggan, to Mexico for six months to learn Spanish. Duggan later went on to become a key member of the Mission Band.

Although the Mission Band was abruptly "disbanded," the legendary work of these priests earned for them the highest respect and gratitude of concerned Catholics, especially Mexican Americans. This point of reference to the Band preserves an important part of Church history that merits remembrance and retelling.

Fr. Phillip's compassion and love for economically poor minority group children whom he received every summer at his Camp Sunshine is a stark contrast to the present day sexual abuse of children by clergy we read about today. In addition to his positive influence on children, the mentoring and nurturing he gave towards the formation of young seminarians merits great admiration and respect. Each summer Fr. Philipps added mightily to the maturity and cultural sensitivity of young men who later provided distinguished levels of service and leadership of their own inside and outside the institutional Church

Recognizing the value different orders of religious women provide to the well being of local parishes, Jerry Cox warmly describes how Fr. Philipps negotiated a contract with the spirited Sisters of Social Service to add their pioneering Jane Adams-Hull House type of outreach with immigrants and at-risk populations living at St. Mary's Parish. Recalling their success in doing "old fashioned stuff" reminds us once again of how much and how well our Catholic populations are served by these legions of talented, generous and self-sacrificing Sisters who give so much to improving the lot of people who might otherwise be left behind in extreme poverty or marginalization. In addition to describing their valuable work, the author includes the names of these venerable sisters for us to remember.

As a seasoned manager and executive wearing different hats, Cox also gives well-deserved credit to another important group of religious sisters, The Holy Name Sisters who made available a quality base of education at St. Mary's Elementary School beginning in 1886. Over the years, these Sisters provided successful learning experiences to all children who crossed their doors, especially their last and largest group of second language learners living in the Parish, the Mexican American population.

Attributing much of his own success to the mentoring he received from Fr. Philipps, Jerry shares with us the impact and fruits of is own work as the social idealist he also became. In addition to advanced work at Catholic University of America, Washington, D.C., Jerry ascended to higher and higher positions with Catholic Social Service, Hanna Boys Center for delinquent boys, and as Monsignor and Chancellor in the new Diocese of Santa Rosa.

It is in the Santa Rosa Diocese that Jerry goes on to nurture an abundance of togetherness with the Mexican community that began at St. Mary's Parish and that never diminishes or stops. Whether wearing the Roman Collar or not, Jerry Cox was always there to provide support and friendship to foster the well being of all groups, but none as extensively and closely as with the Mexican and Mexican-American people. His success has much to inform all who seek to reach or work with the rapid increase of Hispanics now living throughout the United States, especially beyond the traditional five Southwestern States where they once located.

Over the years, Jerry has found true love and peace in the arms of his wonderful wife, Kathy and growing family. He remains active in his community, is well liked and close to an active network of old friends and colleagues. Like his mentor, Jerry moves comfortably between the poor and the rich, enjoys gourmet food, vintage drinks, and a good joke. He remains strongly committed to issues of equity and justice and always brings his own coal to coalitions engaged in service to the poor and oppressed.

At a time when the Catholic Church is desperately in need of heroes, this book is a must read, especially for all who long for a time when relationships were durable, trustworthy and worthy of a friendly nod, or thumbs up. This work reflects genuine compassion, feeling and insight, written by a person who has a deep and abiding understanding of the Catholic Church and love of people, especially those who merit remembrance. Told with great humor and wit, this book rescues Father Philipps' irreplaceable life story from the dust bins of history and helps us discover the life of a remarkable, unapologetic, and practical agitator, who gave us all a nice, but sometimes bumpy ride.

Dr. Herman Gallegos
Galt, California

INTRODUCTION

❧⦿❧

$\mathcal{T}$his is a tale of two Roman Catholic priests, one in his middle 20's and newly ordained; the other, a French Alsatian senior clergyman recently retired from long years of service to the poor. The first was myself assigned in June 1950 to St. Mary of The Immaculate Church, in West Oakland, California. The second one was Rev. Charles Philipps of Stundwillder, French Alsace. I was assigned as an Assistant Pastor following my ordination in June 16, 1950; Charles, a Pastor Emeritus who continued to reside at St. Mary's rectory. I came from a fairly well known and connected family in Oakland. My grandfather John Cox arrived penniless at Ellis Island, New York, from County Roscommon, Ireland, landed in Oakland, and after several careers as street car conductor and police officer, he and three other Irishmen started a successful mortuary business, Freeman, Cox, Roach, and Kenny. My maternal grandfather, Michael Coakley, and brother James had also immigrated from County Cork. Ireland, operated a successful meat market that served wealthy customers in Piedmont. My father, John Cox, followed a mortuary career, was active in fraternal organizations, and ran for political office (Alameda County Coroner) and lost twice, even after parading his set of triplet 3 year old boys and girl with "Cox For Coroner" sweaters at every union picnic and political gathering in Alameda County. So while my upbringing was definitely upper middle class, I found myself assigned to Oakland's oldest neighborhoods and oldest church, an area of fading Victorian houses, resident hotels of social security pensioners, a Skid Row, and ethnic grocery stores and cafes, with a Black and Mexican population. The parish church community reflected the neighborhood of elderly white parishioners and Mexican families. My seminary training had not prepared me to deal with either the culture of the neighborhood nor the language. One early incident describes this very clearly. I visited a family in an old run down house to talk with a father of six children about arranging for a housekeeper following the death of his wife, During our conversation he told one of his daughters, "Get the padre a taco". The only taco I had ever eaten and was a corn tortilla filled with meat, lettuce, avocado, and dripping with salsa. To my amazement the young girl returned from the kitchen with a cold flour tortilla rolled up with cold beans! That was my introduction to the tacos of the poor. However, of my 23 years as a Catholic priest I recall these five years in West Oakland as the most interesting and exciting. I was starting my career as a parish priest. Charles was quietly wrapping up his after urban assignments in San Jose, San Francisco, and Oakland, as well as rural ones in Stockton, Pinole, and Sebastopol. He had finished his active years as pastor of St. Mary's also in 1950, completing 39 years of church assignments, a 20 year advocate for small farmers, and the founder of a summer camp for poor White, Mexican, and Black children in Sonoma County, California. Now with his hearing fading, his health slowly deteriorating, his tall frame and broad shoulders slightly drooping, he requested retirement and permission to reside at St. Mary's. For five years I lived with him, listened to his clerical experiences, became his chauffeur, and later his nurse as his health began to worsen. Although our paths separated with my transfer to graduate school and other church assignments, my image of the priesthood, the Catholic Church and community, and the battle for social justice was shaped by these daily encounters with him. My later research into his life through archives and personal interviews of his friends deepened my respect and love of this "radical peasant". He remains still a force in my years as a social activist both in and out of the priesthood. So this story is both his and mine. I have attempted to describe the creative influence which he had on my life and that of countless others as well as award him the recognition as one of the most vocal advocates for rural social action in the 1930's-1940's, an acknowledgement that is long overdue him. Few European immigrant priests achieved the status and influence that he did. He bridged the cultural language gap successfully and even humorously during 47 years of his priestly career.

The village of Stundwiller, located in the northeastern corner of Alsace, France, is laid out in the form of an elongated wishbone with the Rue Arriere and the Rue Principalle paralleling each other from the town's main entrance. Both streets run for five blocks and end at a small hill that features the imposing and rebuilt Church of St. George, the patron of this very Catholic village. The church was completely destroyed in the bombardments and tank battles of World War II. Alongside the church lies the parish cemetery where Charles' parents are buried. Below the hill sit the town's Mayor's office, an ancient police station, and a small community center. The two story houses built in typical Alsatian design of a stucco first floor and wood-faced second floors are built up against old unused barns. Vegetable plots mark the front yards. Only a few residents today farm the rolling hills surrounding the town. Today most people cross the Rhine River into Germany for well-paying jobs.

In 1286 the Parish of Stundwiller covered a vast territory connecting nine other villages as the ancient possession of the Abbey of Wiessenburg. Later it was handed over to the bishop of Spires. The village population increased from 17 families of twenty-eight adults and forty-nine children to 595 inhabitants in 1826. This last census recorded the largest population in Stundwiller's history. Today about 90 families occupy the village which is surrounded by small hills of farmland which are maintained by large corporate agricultural interests. East to West a long line of round concrete pillboxes, now cracked and vine covered, stretch out along the German border, remnants of the famous Maginot Line erected as fortifications against future German invasions following World War I. The soil of Stundwiller has been steeped in the blood since the invasion of the German tribes, Vandals, Goths, Franks, Alemani, Roman legions, the French-Prussian War, World War I, and finally World War II. Stundwiller was lost and then regained by American troops during World War II through the famous armored offensive "Norwind" in January 1944. A fifteen-foot concrete crucifix stands like a silent sentry across from a Maginot pillbox as a memorial to the Philipps' family.

Charles's parents Aloise Philipps and Marqurite Strasser were married in Stundwiller on September 11, 1861. He was 25 and she 30 years old. Charles from nearby Aschbach Bas Rhein and Margaret from Stundwiller. The marriage produced four children Marie Philipps (September 19,1873), Josephine (June 14, 1876), Aloise (March 12, 1878), and Charles (September 17, 1881). Aloise, the father, was classified as a "cordonnier domiclie", a shoemaker who owned only eight acres of his own and probably rented others. Stundwiller farmers in those days farmed by hand producing wheat, oats, beans, potatoes, and other grains. They also raised livestock. The pork products of Stundwiller enjoyed a prized reputation throughout Alsace.

Aloise and Margurite must have set a very pious and religious atmosphere in their home. All four children entered the service of the church. Marie Margurite at 18 entered the Sisters of Divine Providence of St. John Basel. The Abbe Jean Martin Maye founded this religious community in 1762 with seven young women from Stundwiller as the original members. Abbe Maye's words to them were,"Your principal spiritual work will be the instruction of anyone who needs instruction, both children and adults, with your primary attention to those who are ill." Margurite took the religious name of "Sister of the Sacred Heart" on April 22, 1891. She taught at various schools for forty-seven years, retiring in 1948 at St. Joseph's Retreat House where she died February 25, 1959.

Josephine followed her sister into the same community on May 24, 1893, choosing Marie Adele as her religious name. She also taught at various posts for thirty-nine years until she suffered an illness, which forced her to retire. She died at age 67 on July 21, 1943.

The Philipps' sons Alloise and Charles were attracted to the Roman Catholic priesthood. Alloise, ordained on July 24, l904, became a much beloved and well-known pastor who rode a bicycle through his parish and introduced bingo. Retiring due to illness on January 1961, he passed away at Marienthal on November 2, l957.

Following his elementary school studies in Stundwiller, Charlie completed his secondary and college schooling at the College of Sainte Marie Belfort and Basaucon where he received his French Baccalaureate degree in 1903. His next stop along his education route was the University of Milan, Italy, from 1903 to 1905 where he received a Licentiate in German, and then on to the University of Friboug, Switzerland, from 1905 to 1908 where he majored in Philosophy. Charlie spent six semesters there at the university majoring in languages, German, Italian, Spanish, and English. His philosophy course was more of a liberal arts track. According to his correspondence he went to Fribourg specifically to learn English and while continuing his English studies, he became a teacher of German and English as well as manager of sports in the French College of Fribourg. It was probably at Fribourg where he made his decision to study for the Catholic priesthood. From 1908 to 1911 he entered the famous Dominican seminary and training center for priests of Switzerland and other parts of Europe, the Albertinum, which was staffed by an international faculty of Dominican priest scholars from France, Germany, Italy, and Spain. The city of Fribourg was also the seat of the Bishopric of Fribourg, Lausanne, and Geneva and was the center of Swiss Catholicism with about two-thirds of the population speaking French and another one-third German. As the capital of the Swiss Canton of the same name, Fribourg is located in an elevated plain rising from the flat land of the West, through the hill region and up on to the Pre-Alps in the south and east.

The city of Fribourg consists of two sections, the very modern architecture, boulevards and smart shops that traverse an upper ridge, and the medieval fairly-like section interlaced with ornamental fountains on cobblestone streets that spill gracefully down to the River Sarne which churns through this ancient site of fourteen fortified towers, gates, the Berne covered wooden bridge from 1250, a water -balance funicular connecting Old Fribourg with the stone faced plaza of the town hall (Hotel de Ville, 1522). The jumble of red tile roof tops and narrow houses graced by artful spires are overseen by the majestic gothic towers of St. Nicolas Cathedral that presides over this medieval pageantry like a protective parent. Charlie must have been wrapped up in this mantle of medieval magic as he peeked out of his window or walked around these streets experiencing such sights as St. Nicolas Cathedral (13-15 th centuries), the Franciscan Church (Eglise de Cordeliers, 1281), the Church of St. Maurice (1255), as well the ancient gateways with their 13th-17th century ramparts which originally surrounded the city. Charlie was always exceedingly proud of his Fribourg studies. He looked down on Roman universities' Doctorates earned by aspiring clerics in Roman Theology Schools. As for history studied in Switzerland, he once remarked, "There at Fribourg we studied real history, not that god damned Dago history!"

Charlie's citizenship, like his native Alsace, had bounced back and forth between Germany and France. Incorporated into France through the French Revolution in 1789, Alsace was divided into two departments: Haut Rin (Upper Rhine) and Bas Rin (Lower Rin). Following the Franco-German War in 1870, Alsace was annexed to Germany but returned to France after World War I. The loss of Alsace-Lorraine to Germany from 1870 to 1914 was a cause of much anti-German feeling in France. Under German rule Alsatians were denied effective self government until 1902. Thousands of people protested, and those who considered themselves French immigrated to France. Following French annexation after World War I, the French government attempted to substitute state run schools for the traditional Church school and suppress the seventy-five percent of the newspapers written in German. World War II saw the country ceded to Germany again and finally returned to France in 1945.

Writing to Archbishop Riordan of San Francisco on August 17th, 1910, to request admission as a student for the priesthood for the Archdiocese of San Francisco, Charlie mentioned that he did not belong to the diocese of Strasbourg, his home diocese in France, since he had made his classical studies in France, renounced his rights as a German citizen, and acquired French citizenship. "For these reasons," he wrote, "according to the political laws that rule Alsace, the Roman Catholic Bishop of Strasbourg is forbidden to ordain me for his diocese." Charlie mentioned in his letter that in Archbishop Riordan's acceptance of him, "I saw it only as a sign of divine providence for such a large field of activity as I was anxiously looking for, being completely free and about beginning my last year in theology." He also mentioned that "he has a mind for teaching and is fond of languages and history." He had joined the Columbia Society, an American student organization, "in order to have more opportunity of practicing English and getting acquainted with American manners." He ended his letter to Archbishop Riordan by stating that he "hoped it would not be too hard and take too long to adapt himself to the new clergy, people and customs and that with God's help and your Grace's kind counsels, he should soon be able to do some good in the vineyard of the Lord." Archbishop Riordan and the Archdiocese of San Francisco got a "good deal" in adopting Charlie. The Rev. Regent of the seminary, the Theologisches Konvict Albertinum, Dr. J. B. Muller, wrote to Archbishop Riordan saying that in Charlie, " Your Grace will have a thoroughly good and useful priest of good character." Dr. Muller got down to the practical subject of tuition costs and assumed that Riordan will agree to pay them. He explained that bishops of American students usually send $200 a year per student, but that European students adopted into American Dioceses receive only 200 francs and money for the passage to America. Had Charlie known this later he probably would have demanded a refund.

In a June 13, 1911, letter to Archbishop Riordan, Charlie informed him that he will be ordained a priest at Fribourg on July 9th and will say his first Mass on July 16th in his own parish church of Stundwiller. He must have been short of cash, for he requested that the Archbishop send him "about 40 Mass stipends."

Charlie was ordained to the Roman Catholic priesthood on July 9th, 1911, in the seminary chapel of the Albertinum and said his first Mass on July 11th, at the Stundwiller parish of St. George. The parish priest at the time, Rev. Nicolas Grussenmeyer, described the celebration and festivities: " The celebration turned out to be a magnificent one. All the houses in the village were beautifully decorated with flags, wreaths and triumphal arches. It was a real Via Triumphalis from the parental home to the church which was filled to the rafters to welcome home one whom they remembered as a little boy running through the Rue Principale, now dressed in priestly vestments for his first Mass." "This celebration," continued the priest, "will be long remembered by the members of the parish. July 16th in the year 1911 will be engraved in the memory of the parish Stundwiller-Oberroedern."

The newly ordained Alsatian cleric, age 30, boarded the Holland Line ship, the <u>Nieuw</u> <u>Amersterdam</u>, at Rollerdam, Holland, arriving at Ellis Island, New York City, on August 21, 1911. He next boarded an overland train out of Grand Central Station and began his westward journey.

In the construction of the transcontinental railroad, Oakland, California, was chosen as its Western terminus. Trains from the East and Midwest ended at the Southern Pacific Railroad's pier in Oakland known as the "S.P. Mole". Passengers boarded a ferry boat and crossed the San Francisco Bay, docking at the famous Ferry Building in San Francisco. As he ascended the large staircase to the top deck, Charlie's eyes wandered over the large San Francisco Bay in amazement. Other than crossing the Atlantic Ocean, he had never see such a large body of water. Soon he would embark after a twenty minute trip to the San Francisco side and up to the Chancery Office where he would meet Archbishop Riordan for the first time and receive his first parish assignment. Although conversant in French, German, Italian, and his native Alsatian dialect, his acquired spoken English proved quite adequate. While his fluency improved over the years, he wondered about his ability to fit in. He was an Alsatian farm boy educated in universities in Milan and Fribourg. His clerical peers would be Irish born and local American trained clergy. Although his priestly career would prove to be a successful one, he never lost his Franco-German accent, his continental savoir-faire, nor his identity with agriculture. While he would return to Alsace only twice in his 47 years in the USA, he kept in touch with the small Alsatian community of the Bay Area.

ALOYSE PHILIPPS

MARGUERITE STRASSER

PHILIPPS FAMILY HOME
45 RUE PRINCIPALE
STUNDWILLER, ALSACE

REVEREND ALOYSE PHILIPPS
1878-1952
GOLDEN JUBILEE CELEBRATION

SISTER OF THE SACRED HEART (MARIE MARGURITE PHILIPPS)

1873-1959

SISTER MARIE-ADELE (JOSEPHINE PHILIPPS)
1876-1943

LABORS IN THE VINEYARD

◦◦◯◦◦

*T*he geographical size of the Archdiocese of San Francisco at the time of Charlie's arrival was enormous: 16,856 square miles of 11 counties. All of the territories and counties that made up the Archdiocese resembled a huge fan with San Francisco at the center. From San Francisco it ran north to Marin, Sonoma Mendocino counties, northeast to Napa, Lake Counties, across the San Francisco Bay to Oakland and Alameda, Contra Costa and Santa Clara, and East to San Joaquin and Stanislaus counties. With the exception of San Francisco, the East Bay, parts of Marin and San Mateo counties, the Archdiocese could qualify as a rural diocese at this time with agriculture playing a major role in the economy.

Charlie's early priesthood years began as an assistant pastor in the Mission District, Irish neighborhood of St. Peter's Church, San Francisco, where he stayed only four months, September to December 1911. He was transferred south to San Jose where he stayed only one month. Charlie must have enjoyed a considerable amount of respect with the Archbishop to be able to request a change of assignment. Assistant pastors usually enjoyed very little influence in effecting their own assignment changes. However, Charlie wrote to the Archbishop asking for a change because a Father Lally "was not fit to live with."

He returned to San Francisco and was appointed to the well-to-do parish of St. Bridget, located at Broadway and Van Ness Avenue. St. Bridget's included the wealthiest neighborhoods of Nob Hill and Tele-

graph Hill, the neighborhoods of San Francisco society. Charlie may
have been the son of Alsatian peasants, but he was also a highly educated and traveled European who was always able to move comfortably between the poor and the rich, to turn breakfast pancakes for poor kids at
his Sunshine Camp as well as to enjoy gourmet food and vintage wines.
At St. Bridget's he enjoyed four years of pastoral work from 1912 to 1916
where he also made some lasting friendships with wealthy parishioners
whom he would later "tap" to help him with his Sunshine Camp.

The next four years saw him across the San Francisco Bay to the
parishes of St. Anthony's in East Oakland, 1916 to 1918, and the nearby
Church of St. Mary's in West Oakland, 1918 to 1920 to which he would
return as pastor years later – the future scene of some of his greatest
achievements. Charlie's correspondence revealed an interesting letter
written on November 9, 1917, to the Adjutant General, War Department, Washington D.C., in which he applied for a position as a chaplain
in the U.S. Army. The letter is very brief and contains no reference of
his ever having discussed the possibility of a military chaplaincy with
his church supervisors. The correspondence file does not contain any
response or follow-up.

In the clerical folklore of the predominantly Irish clergy of these
early years of the Archdiocese, a curate or new pastor accepted his fate
of being stationed in the far away rural outposts of Stockton, Tracy, or
Ukiah and then gradually working his way back to the mother city of
San Francisco. A pastorship in the "City" was every priest's dream and
a sign that one had influence with the Archbishop's office as well as a
history of upright behavior. County Deans who represented the Archbishop in those remote areas (in these days of the two lane highway, it
was probably a 5-6 hour trip to San Francisco) lived far enough away
not to be bothered by inquisitive representatives of the Archbishop. It
would have taken a major clerical scandal for someone to have come
that far. Consequently, the pastors and Deans in these areas ruled very
autocratically. At the same time, the Archbishop and his advisors would
not hesitate to assign a "problem" priest, the alcoholic or insubordinate
cleric, to one of these autocratic pastors to straighten them out. Many
an assistant pastor dreaded the day he might be sent to one of these for

purification and rehabilitation through insult, house arrest, and harassment. The stories of the legendary pastor of Petaluma, James Kiely, and the long line of curates that were sent to him for rehabilitation could fill pages. Kiely, Irish born, once boasted that he was the oldest priest in the Archdiocese. When he was reminded that a Czechoslovakian priest by the name of Krump in San Francisco was 4 years older than he, Kiely retorted "...he doesn't count, he's a foreigner!"

In the 1930's, Tracy, California, a pastor named Mills, became frustrated at the large number of pennies showing up in the Sunday collections and vowed he would take them out of circulation. So every three months he would take a suitcase load of rolled one cent coins down to San Francisco and deposit them in the bank, hoping they would not make their way back to town.

Charlie had become aware of a large Portuguese community both in Oakland and in the rural areas of the Archdiocese, as well as of his inability to speak Portuguese. He was fluent in German, French, Italian, and his own native language of Alsace-Lorraine. He always had a love and ability for languages. Consequently, he combined a six month trip home to Alsace with a five month stopover in Lisbon to study Portuguese. His letter on November 3, 1920, to Archbishop Riordan described his arriving in the Portugal capital "after a tiresome trip, owing to a railroad strike in the country." He first paid his respects to the then "Patriarch" of Lisbon who did not give him a friendly reception. When Charlie informed him of his intention of enrolling in language and history classes at the national university, the Patriarch held up the Code of Canon Law which forbade priests from studying at State Universities, unless they secured explicit permission from their bishops. Charlie requested such a letter from Riordan at his earliest convenience. "Meanwhile," he continued, "I shall occupy my time by taking private lessons, by conversations, and by reading."

Charlie's interest and personal dedication to learn Portuguese was a rarity amongst most clergymen that I knew in my twenty-three years in the clergy. Most of us were probably very ignorant of Portuguese parishioners, particularly the men who hung out in front of church while their wives and families worshiped inside. Most of the Portuguese were immigrants from the Azores Islands who, like other immigrants, came to the U.S. because of poverty. As a group they were uneducated, spoke little if any English, and operated their benevolent Holy Ghost societies apart from the institutional church. Irish pastors would become enraged when the local society came to arrange the annual Holy Ghost celebrations with pageantry of Holy Ghost Queens and court, parades, and a dinner with the famous Portuguese "Sopa." The pastor would not see many of the participants in his church afterwards. The prevailing negative attitude of the clergy was mainly due to a lack of knowledge/background of the people's history, culture, and certainly language. There were a few native Portuguese priests, but not enough to minister to the large Portuguese community. The mentality of the U.S. Church in those days was to establish "national" parishes staffed by native speaking clergy where services, worship, and religious festivals could be conducted in the home language. And so, English speaking clergy as a whole did not feel obligated to learn another foreign language to enrich their ministry. They reflected the mentality of the times that the immigrant should become familiar with the culture and learn English. Charlie was an exception. Because of his unique ability to relate to various groups of people, he personally embodied the philosophy of modern language acquisition, that one had to absorb the culture of a people in acquiring their language. Years alter he would write to Archbishop Mitty, criticizing and bemoaning the inability of the clergy to communicate with the then large and growing Mexican-Spanish speaking population of the Archdiocese. He remarked that priests in Europe were all multilingual, that the clergy of the Southwest had to learn Spanish, but that St. Patrick's Seminary, the major seminary of the Archdiocese, sent out its men unable to communicate a word in Spanish. He also met with opposition from the Chancery Office in getting permission for his assistant John Duggan at St. Mary's, Oakland, to live in Mexico for six months in order to improve his Spanish and learn the culture of Mexico. He told the Archbishop that he was "not asking for a vacation for Duggan, but a leave which he was happy to finance."

Following his language internship in Lisbon, Charlie traveled home to Alsace. During his visit he wrote to Monsignor Cantwell, then the

Vicar General of the Archdiocese, that he had taken the "heart cure" at Bad Nauheiim Medical Clinic which was only 150 miles from his home in Alsace, from July first to August eighth. He described the treatment of 18 baths, plenty of rest, and a special diet. He reported that his appetite had improved and that he felt stronger. Also he had begun taking inhalation treatments to cure his sinus problems. These descriptions are the first references of many medical reports and conditions that he would share with the Archbishop. For such a vigorous person, Charlie seems to have been plagued with bad health all of his life. If one were to put all of his health reports together, one might get the picture of a hypochondriac. However, he never complained about his health. He wrote on July first, 1931, that he "had arrived this afternoon and put himself under the care of a leading physician, a Doctor Groedel, who had also treated San Francisco's Archbishop Riordan at one time." Charlie wrote on August 27, 1931, thanking Archbishop Hanna for his telegram and the Papal Blessing for his family. He was feeling much better and enjoying his father in his "young old age" and finding him "mentally fit."

Upon his return form Europe, Charlie received his first appointment as Pastor of the rural parish of Hughson in San Joaquin Valley, a dairy and farming community with a large Portuguese population of farmers. Here he made his first contacts with farmers with whom he would be involved in his Catholic Rural Life activities and his cooperative efforts with The Church of The Brethren's "Heifers for Europe" project to replenish the cattle herds that had been destroyed in World War II. Hughson was the first of four rural appointments he would receive for two years, followed by St. Patrick's in Rodeo-Pinole, Contra Costa County, where he became the first resident pastor for six years, and St. Gertrude Parish, stockton, where after one year he had to relinquish the administration of the parish due to heart problems. His letter to the Archbishop described the various ailments he suffered from. He had developed a serious sinus problem as a result of hay fever and was experiencing many sleepless nights. Also the heat and humidity of Stockton caused an "unbelievable" irritation to the tissues of his rectum and trouble with varicose veins. He enclosed medical reports from two doctors who had cared for him in the previous fifteen years. He also reported that in nine months he had paid off $500 of the parish debt and had increased the Sunday school attendance from 200 to 400 children.

Upon the news of his transfer from St. Gertrude's, a Stockton surgeon named R. T. McGurk, M.D., wrote and informed Archbishop Hanna that "the removal of Father Philipps would be a grave mistake for various reasons." His work in going out and recruiting children for Sunday school classes was remarkable. He had developed a well-organized plan among prominent Protestant and Catholics to reduce a large portion of the debt which had been out–standing for a long time. Doctor McGurk described Charlie as a "man of conviction and courage, one who has been invited into the homes and tables of the financially and socially elite of the town. His early removal will be viewed with resentment and regret by thinking Catholics and Protestants alike." Apparently, McGurk was not privy to Charlie's medical conditions brought on by the environment of Stockton.

Finally, in July of 1930, Charlie was appointed Pastor of St. Sebastian's Church, Sebastopol, near Santa Rosa, a farming and agricultural community in Sonoma County, California, where his love and affinity with farmers during the Depression would project him into action and advocacy for his agricultural flock.

PINKO PRIEST

$\mathcal{F}$or all of Charlie's European sophistication, he considered and prided himself on being a peasant. Invited to address the California State Chamber of Commerce regarding the return of Armed Force Veterans to farming and ranching on March 1, 1945, Charlie opened his remarks by saying, "I dare assert that I can speak with more authority on farming than any of you here present on account of my active and direct contact with the manure pile. From eight to fourteen years of age I got my bare feet into that warm, oozy stuff with its pungent smell. I pulled manure and litter out of the stable with a two pronged hoe, and after that stuff had been plowed under for a few weeks, my father, like a good peasant, would pick up a handful of it, crumble it, and declare that the soil smelled sweet and fat."

If a successful pastor is able to identify with his people, Charlie's peasant background made him ideal for his assignments in agricultural areas like Stockton in the San Joaquin Valley, Houston, a dairy community of Portuguese farmers, and finally Sebastopol, a community of small apple growers on the west side of the Santa Rosa Valley, Sonoma County, where he was appointed pastor of St. Sebastian's Catholic Church during the Great Depression years of 1929-1936. Saint Sebastian was an early Christian Church martyr who, tied to a stake, was executed by a hail of arrows through his chest. Charlie would eventually feel the sting of people's anger during his seven years here.`

Located in the Western side of Sonoma County, the area around

Sebastopol with its slow rise of hills reminded the new pastor of the topography of his native Alsace. Early pioneers had come to California to find their fortunes in the gold fields, but others found their fortunes in the rich soil of Sonoma county which could produce almost any kind of fruit or grain. These early settlers were a rich ethnic mix of Italians, Portuguese, Swiss, Irish, British, Germans, and Chinese.

Wheat was the first king of crops in 1884 of which Sonoma County produced 2,100,000 bushels and exported 2,000,000. Western Sonoma County also produced a thriving berry industry. As one travelled through their area, his eyes focused on the long vast fields of hop fields with their 20 foot vines that stood alongside of their church-like hop kilns that dotted the landscape. Sugar beets were also grown for profit.

But it was the Gravenstein apple which made Sebastopol nationally famous. Russian colonists had established a fort (the present Ft. Ross) and farm on the Sonoma Coast as an agricultural center to grow and feed their colony in Sitku, now Alaska. One of the fruits which they introduced was the "Grav" apple which was adopted by local farmers, particularly a Nathaniel Griffith who proved that the apple was a viable commercial crop. By 1920 Sonoma County had 27,000 acres in cultivation. In the middle of the Depression Sebastopol was shipping 50,000 tons of dried apples and 1.5 million boxes of fresh fruit annually.

Luther Burbank, the world famous botanist and plant breeder, moved from the East to Sonoma County in 1875 where he spent the remainder of his life on an experimental Sebastopol farm. There he developed 100 new varieties of plums and prunes, 50 different types of lilies, and 10 varieties of commercial berries.

It was no wonder that Charlie, another immigrant to the scene, and an Alsatian peasant was thrilled to be appointed to this rich center of farming and agriculture.

Gaye Le Barron, the noted columnist of the <u>Santa Rosa Press Democrat</u>, in her historical volume <u>Santa Rosa: A Nineteenth Century Town</u> described the origin of Sebastopol, originally called Pine Grove. "Sebastopol" originated in a fight between a man named Hibbs and a Jeff Stevens who chased Hibbs into a general store owned by one John Dougherty. When Stevens was refused entry to the store, disappointed onlookers cried that it was "Hibbs' Sebastopol," that being the time during the Crimean War when the allies were attacking and getting nowhere.

Like most farming communities, Sebastopol citizens were conservative, independent, and rugged individualists. The Roman Catholic community consisted of Italian, Portuguese, and Irish families who were also victims of the anti-Catholic attitudes of this era. Surprisingly, Charlie's appointment created a second Reverend Philipps in town, the other being the local Methodist Pastor, Reverend Philipps. The Post Office frequently mixed up their mail. Charlie and the Methodist pastor would exchange mail pieces in front of the bank, the local citizens' meeting place. Charlie used to say that he "didn't mind getting Rev. Philipps' mail, as long as he didn't get his bills." Charlie's sense of humor and his evident humanity gradually broke down the town's anti-Catholic sentiment, and soon Catholics and Protestants were talking to each other.

As the new Pastor, Charlie witnessed and experienced the Depression in Sebastopol. The parish received very little income; he could not receive a salary, but lived off his farmer and ranch parishioners' gifts of eggs, meat, vegetables, milk, and fruit. Like a true European peasant, he organized a group of Italian stonemasons to build a stone cold cellar in the rear of the priest's house where he could store his donated food. Parishioners called the cellar "Father Philipps' Bastille" because it was so strongly built. Years later, when the old church property was sold, it took a bulldozer to dismantle it.

According to Ed Treigero, a Sebastopol native and retired real estate broker, the unorganized apple ranchers were fighting among themselves and rushing their green fruit to market to beat their competitors. "Philipps", remarked Treijero, "was a controversial guy who had very strong opinions. You either hated him or loved him. He used to show up at farmers' meetings and tell them what to do, especially to develop a co-operative for their own protection." He remembered his apple grower father coming home from a farmers' meeting muttering that he wished "Father Philipps would stay home." In later years Charlie stated that he had influenced the establishment of the famous Sebastopol Apple Co-op.

A farmer organization, the Farmers' Protective League, was formed with Charlie's involvement. The League became very active in rallying farmers and surrounding communities against the bank foreclosures on small farmers. One famous case revolved around the pending bank foreclosure of a retired 75 year-old Methodist Minister, James L. Case, who owned a 50 acre apple/cherry orchard on Mirabel Road. In 1933 Case was able to pay his taxes, but not the payment on his $14,000 mortgage. In the summer of 1933, Analy Savings Bank foreclosed on him and scheduled a sale of his ranch for July 14th.

A mass meeting of farmers was called by the Farmers' Protective League at Case's farm where Charlie also spoke. The San Francisco News of Thursday, July 13, 1933, declared "Sunday's meeting on the steps of the Case home marked the reappearance of Stitt Wilson of Berkeley, an old time Socialist leader of the evangelical-preacher type." Mr. Wilson was badly quoted in some of the newspapers, but his speech was fiery enough, and he had the backing of a Catholic priest of Sebastopol, the Reverend Charles Philipps."

"A Priest Fights for Farmers" was the title of the long editorial in The San Francisco Call Bulletin by Fremont Older, President and Editor. "Reverend Father Charles Philipps, who officiates over a small parish in Sebastopol, Sonoma County, is creating quite a stir in that small town by expressing the cause of the beleaguered apple growers." The editorial continued to state that "Philipps is not interested in the corporation farmer, but the one who owns and operates his own farm." Charlie attacked those Governmental plans to relieve the problems of farmers. "Those who were the first to sponsor these bills and agreements were all those who, in the past, made money farming the farmers. I refer to the packers, carriers, brokers, and advertising units – in other words, the whole fascist organization who so lately were exploiting the farmer, have now turned an about face and are leading him out of the desert of chaos into the promised land of prosperity. They had the brains in the past, but either forgot their multiplication tables or overlooked the Ten Commandments with emphasis on the Seventh, "Thou Shalt Not Steal".

In his May 31, 1937, letter to Archbishop Mitty, Charlie sent him a copy of his statement made before the President's Special Farm Tenancy Committee hearing on January 12, 1937. The Associated Farmers of California, whom Charlie would dub the "ASS-ociated Farmers", reported on Charlie's testimony by saying, "Reverend Charles Philipps, a Catholic priest from Sebastopol, said small farmers were paying more to their workers than were large operators. He attacked the State Chamber of Commerce and the Associated Farmers." "The problems," he said, "could not be solved by sawed off shotguns. The policies of these organizations were anti-economical." He concluded his remarks by attacking the wine industry, the milk industry, and fruit growers in general.

Back in Sebastopol, when Analy Bank directors refused to change their minds about Case, even after interventions from prominent political figures including President Roosevelt, the sale of Case's property went ahead. Charlie joined the thousands of farmers from Northern California on the steps of the Sonoma County Court House, Santa Rosa, to prevent Case's eviction. During the rally the news of local Judge Hillary Comstock's injunction to halt the sale was announced to the cheering crowd. Shortly afterward, the Jones Act, a state mortgage moratorium, was passed in the California Legislature.

Farm foreclosures in the United States during the 1920's and 1930's reached heights never previously or since exceeded. One of the most dreaded aspects of the Great Depression in rural areas was that of farm foreclosures and loss of farms which reduced farm families and landowners to the status of tenants or farm laborers, and in the depths of the Depression, to walk bread lines and soup kitchens. From 1921 to 1940 over 96,000 farms were foreclosed each year. 1933 was the worst, with 200,000 foreclosures. In California, foreclosure rates averaged 30,200 in 1932 to 13,000 in 1940, with 1933 experiencing the highest number during this period, 38,000.

Due to the outcry of farmers and farmer groups in 1933, the Federal Government enacted the Agricultural Adjustment Act with the purpose of raising and stabilizing farm income. From 1933 to 1935, 25 states including California passed legislation which enacted a moratorium on mortgages, thus preventing creditors from foreclosing on farmers who were delinquent with their mortgage payments.

Like in most rural communities in California, the power structure in Sonoma County consisted of landowners, County Supervisors,
judges, and law enforcement. Gaye LeBarron remarked, "Historically
agriculture had been king in Sonoma County. Farmers, particularly
the growers around Santa Rosa and Healdsburg, were the power elite.
They owned substantial acreage, often lived in big houses in towns,
and controlled the politics and social life of their communities. Until
the labor movement of the 1930's, their will was never opposed." Since
agriculture was the dominant force in the community, any perceived
threat to its welfare was co-operatively opposed by the entire political structure. While Charlie was admired for his support of farmers,
many of his farmer parishioners were upset by his open support of farm
worker organizing. One prominent Sebastopol grower once told him,
"If he wasn't a Catholic priest, he would have been tarred and feathered
a long time ago."

The threat to a Catholic priest may have been an implied one, but to
organizers of farm workers in Sonoma County, the threats were carried
out. "Farmers in the state lobbied Sacramento for anti-picketing laws,
burned crosses outside of labor camps, and organized quasi-military
forces." This state-wide militancy of farmers gave birth to a state-wide
organization called the Associated Farmers of California. Jack Green,
a Santa Rosa sign painter, and Solomon Netzberg, a chicken rancher,
were forcibly kidnapped from their homes by a band of vigilantes and
brought to a Santa Rosa warehouse, where buckets of tar and chicken
feathers were poured over their stripped bodies. Charlie had previously
provided Green with a sanctuary "hide-out" in the parish house when
the farmer groups were searching for him.

Charlie wrote to Archbishop Mitty on November 3, 1933: "Last
March when I was about to organize the Farmers' Protective League,
you kindly gave me some suggestions and information to guide me in
my work. Whenever I took a stand, whether in regard to co-operatives
or farm foreclosures, I used the Popes' Encyclicals in my arguments. It
is very effective and direct social action." He continued the letter by describing the League's victory in stopping and amicably settling threat-
ened bank foreclosures that amounted to $120,000. The League was

probably the forerunner of the Sebastopol Apple Co-operative, which successfully represented apple growers for years. Charlie frequently stated that he was involved in its founding.

Sebastopol became the platform for all of Charlie's peasant upbringing, particularly his appointment in 1935 as the Archdiocesan Director of the Catholic Rural Life Conference, a member group of the National Catholic Rural Life Conference which advocated and supported the interests of the family farm. Located in Des Moines, Iowa, the National office concentrated most of its attention and activities on Midwest farmers' interests and on national lobbying in Washington, D.C.

While the majority of San Francisco Archdiocesan counties in the 1930's were agricultural areas, farmers' issues and problems were not a priority of the church. Prior to Charlie's appointment, Catholic Rural Life's responsibilities were located in the urban office of Catholic Charities, the Archdiocese's social service organization which served as a convenient hanger for rural social action. Catholic Charities, however, did not have an understanding or relationship to agricultural life and issues. The Rural Life Director whom Charlie succeeded was a Reverend William O'Connor, who had been trained as a social worker at Columbia University, New York. Now in position as Director, Charlie had an official Church organization from which he could address not only Sonoma County issues, but farmers' issues in the whole state as well. These activities continued up to the 1950's prior to his retirement.

Probably no other Catholic voice spoke so loud and forcibly on agricultural social justice issues, wrote as many letters to newspaper editors, assailed enemies of small farmers, and appeared before State and Federal agricultural hearings from the 1930's to the beginnings of the farm worker movement of the 1950's, when new and other religious voices appeared on the scene such as those of the Protestant Churches Migrant Ministry Program, Father James Vizzard, S. J., Ph.D., a nationally recognized agronomist, Father Donald McDonnell, and other local and national figures whose priority was primarily focused on the organization of farm workers, rather than on the interests of the family farm.

While he was actively involved in agricultural issues, Charlie had all of the usual duties of managing a parish community and conducting religious services in his parish which also included the nearby village of Occidental. Peggy Squires had many memories of Charlie. She had come to Sebastopol from San Francisco to live with her elderly aunt, and Peggy drove Charlie in his La Salle to his parishioner farmers to beg for food during the Depression years. They would arrive unannounced and after some conversation, the farmer would ask, "Well, Father Philipps, what can I give you today?", and Charlie would reply, "Oh, some eggs, some meat, and milk." Everyone knew the purpose of Charlie's visit and each actor played his/her role.

Peggy's hopes for a nursing education and career in San Francisco vanished with Charlie playing matchmaker between Peggy and a young man named Bernard Squire, whom Peggy had espied at Sunday Mass. She noticed that he wore a suit and tie and not a pair of overalls like most of the parishioner farmers. Charlie later performed their wedding, opened the priest's house for the bride and bridesmaids to change, and gave them the parish hall for the reception. At that time one of the songs forbidden by the Church for religious services was Gunod's "Ave Maria". When Peggy asked Charlie if it could be sung at the wedding, he walked away saying, "I'm sorry, but I can't hear you!" Peggy and Bernard remained active in Charlie's life until he died. He baptized all their children, witnessed their weddings, and frequently visited their Santa Rosa home.

His Sebastopol activity against bank foreclosures presented him with an opportunity to acquire a 9-acre apple ranch near Mirabel Park on the Russian River. A French woman named Ms. Monvoision, facing foreclosure, turned the mortgage over to Charlie. Writing to Archbishop Mitty about his acquisition, he said "what appealed to me was not the apple orchard (at the present price, it's only good for apple sauce), but the seven room house and four bungalows." The ranch would eventually inspire Charlie to establish Sunshine Camp for poor kids of West Oakland.

Charlie's colorful and active six years in Sebastopol ended with his appointment on July 1, 1936, as Pastor of St. Mary's Church in West Oakland. He expressed his gratitude to Archbishop Mitty for sending him to Oakland "Where his linguistic skills will be used and the financial condition will allow him to continue his rural life work." The Alsatian peasant left the farmers and the farms of Sonoma County for the streets of West Oakland. However, although his new experience would be urban, he would continue his fight for the family farmer.

ST. MARY'S PARISH

⁊he historical roots of St. Mary's Church, Oakland, California, traced themselves back to an original land grant of August 16, 1820, from the King of Spain and his Viceroy in America. Sergeant Luis Maria Peralta, one of the original soldier-explorers, received a grant of 45,000 acres which later constituted both Alameda and Contra Costa Counties. Retiring to Santa Cruz, Peralta divided his land holdings among four sons. Son Vicente received the portion which is now Central Oakland, California. Eventually a small chapel of St. Anthony was built on Seventh Street. When Oakland was incorporated as a Township in 1852, the city fathers donated a block bound by Seventh, Jefferson, Eighth, and Grove Streets for a Catholic church site. Within a year the small chapel of St. Anthony was changed to St. Mary of The Immaculate Conception. Oakland's founding fathers Horace Carpentier, Edson Adams, and Andrew J. Moon had leased 320 acres from Vicente Peralta, which they immediately began to subdivide, sell, and rob Peralta of his holdings. Thus St. Mary's made its start on purloined land violating the ancient moral imperative "non dabitur quod non habet": "you can't donate what you don't own".

Pre-World War II West Oakland of the 1920's and 1930's was a bustling area that provided employment and neighborhood commercial enterprises that reflected its rich European and Asian mix. West Oakland became the end of the line for the Transcontinental Railroad. Passengers from the East and Mid West could disembark at the Oakland Mole, board the Southern Pacific Ferry, disembark at the ferry building, and enter the majesty of "The City." The Southern Pacific Railroad Company's West Oakland rail yards offered hundreds of jobs in its repair yards. Rail transportation serviced the Port of Oakland which shipped California products to foreign markets. The famous Red Train created by the Southern Pacific ran along 7th Street and out to East Oakland; bringing passengers to the San Francisco ferries as well as helping to enrich the lively commercial strip of 7th Street.

The West Oakland economic boom initiated by the railroad created a diverse immigrant community of Greeks, Chinese, Japanese, Italians, Serbians, and Irish. Ethnic groups in West Oakland tended to cluster by country of origin. The section between Castro, Adeline, Market, and 3rd Street was the "Italian Quarter." By 1910 so many Italians lived at 13th and Kirkham Streets that the area was called "Tin Can Alley" because most of the men worked for the local scavenger company. Greeks lived along the railroad tracks and operated businesses on 7th Street. Portuguese lived near St. Joseph's Church at 7th and Chestnut Streets. Bob Valva remembers six different languages spoken on one block. During the 1920's 15 different Greek cafes could be found in West Oakland, which functioned as social clubs and catered to men from different regions of Greece. The Italian Quarter supported at least five grocery and dry goods stores: Clarizio's, Soccos, Sledrio's, Giatani's, and Volpe and Sons, as well as Guido's Fish Market, Genoa and Dante's bakery. The Athens Meat Market, Athens Grocery, and Athens Bakery served the Greek community. A Jewish Deli and a Chinese market provided additional spice.

Several fraternal lodges serving primarily first generation immigrants lined 7th Street and preserved old country traditions and values. One could walk down 7th Street to encounter a Croation Hall, a Jewish Center, and a Portuguese-Azorean IDES, and a German Turnverine Club was located at 3rd and Jackson Street, just outside of West Oakland.

These immigrant groups also carried their native customs into the West Oakland streets. Portuguese in procession celebrated Pentecost with their fiesta in honor of the Holy Ghost; Italian males from Calabria rolled rounds of cheese, playing a cognate of bocce along Market

Street gutters; and, Greeks held candlelight processions around 10th and Brush Street, following Good Friday services. In later years groups of Mexicans celebrated the Christmas Posadas with figures of Joseph and Mary going door to door seeking shelter.

The prosperous 7th Street corridor suffered a serious economic shock with the termination of the Southern Pacific's Red Trains in 1948. Shops and businesses began to close, leaving vacant store fronts. The stillness of the Red Train's shrill whistle echoed the quiet of a neighborhood wake. Likewise, the Southern Pacific's railroad center was witnessing a conversion from steam to diesel locomotives which gradually eliminated their large steam engine maintenance shops which were finally closed in the late 1950's . The ferries continued to run until 1958, causing the cavernous Oakland Mole to become deserted until its demolition in 1960. The number of passenger rail cars out of Oakland declined drastically from 40 trains daily in the 1950's to three in 1960. Those few trains that continued to run left Oakland without the former dining and sleeping cars that had provided steady union jobs to Black Pullman porters.

World War II brought a temporary resurgence of jobs at West Oakland shipyards and related war industry employment at nearby Oakland Army base and Alameda Naval Supply Center which served the Pacific war effort. While both military establishments continued to influence the local economy after the war, they were not a vital part of the West Oakland community. Wartime prosperity allowed first generation immigrants to move out to upscale neighborhoods in East Oakland and Contra Costa County. Their place was taken by Southern Blacks and Mexicans from Mexico and the Southwest states. The port's decline in rail transportation was replaced by the development of auto and truck transportation which required fast corridors to San Francisco. West Oakland, already marked as a slum by Oakland City officials and envied for cheap real estate values, became a natural target. The Nimitz and Cypress elevated freeways may have served the need for rapid access to industries and the Bay bridge, but they tore out blocks of West Oakland homes and whatever neighborhood was left there.

Rosa Maria Escobar reminisced about growing up in West Oakland where she was born. "My mother and father came from Mexico during the Pancho Villa/Zapata period of the Mexican Revolution. My father dressed my grandmother and mother as men, and they rode horseback from Chihuahua to Juarez at night to arrive in El Paso, Texas, where they had only three cents upon entering the USA. The family moved to California and settled in West Oakland where I was born.

"West Oakland in the middle 1930's was comprised mostly of Mexicans, Italians, and a few Irish families. The Fazio and Clarizio families operated Italian grocery stores. The Star Theater, the pool hall on 7th Street, and the Ciudad de Mexico store with Mexican products in the front and a barber shop in the rear served the Mexican community. The neighborhood was peaceful and hospitable. All my girl friends were Italian. It was a working class neighborhood. The Mexican men worked for the Southern Pacific Railroad Company 'en los traques' (on the tracks). St. Mary's was an active center for Mexican teenagers prior to World War II. We formed a club for boys called 'The Darlings' and 'The Debs' for girls. During the war a group of my girl friends coordinated social activities at the YWCA or the 'Braceros', Mexican contract workers who were living in private homes and working or the Southern Pacific Railroad Company. Downtown Oakland featured a number of dance halls with Mexican live band dances: Sands, Sweets, and Persian Gardens, plus another one called The Bucket of Blood because every Saturday night there was usually a fight there. The Hickey rounded out the list of dance halls. Dances took place on Friday and Saturday nights and Sunday afternoons. Sometimes there were one or two going on at the same time with people moving back and forth from one to the other."

When Charlie arrived in West Oakland in 1936, he inherited over eighty years of Oakland Catholic history and a church plan of a 500 seat wood shingle gothic church, a three story priest house, school, upstairs auditorium, social center, and a sisters convent on one square block. The first pastor, a Father Michael Aloysious King in 1886 had recruited the Sisters of the Holy Names of Jesus and Mary from Montreal, Canada, to initiate an elementary school. King secured property adjacent to Lake Merrit where the first contingent of sisters entered a new convent built by St. Mary's parishioners. Father King raised the money by organizing a lottery with his horse and watch as prizes. The convent originally known as the Convent of Our Lady and the Sacred Heart later became the site of a girls' high school and later still a college for women. From 1886 the Holy Names Sisters operated a girls' school at St. Mary's along with the Christian Brothers directing a boys' school. The Brothers withdrew in 1907, leaving the Sisters with the responsibility for both groups.

In his own description of himself as a peasant, Charlie felt more at home in the country with its green fields of cattle, barns, dairies, apple orchards, and vineyards. He could "walk the talk" of the farmer and identify with his struggles. However, his vision was not only rural. He had been an assistant pastor at St. Mary's, Oakland, from 1918 to 1920 when the neighborhood was still a blue collar ethnic working people's neighborhood. However, in his appointment as Pastor in 1936, he witnessed the accumulating dust of West Oakland, the urban poverty, its racial issues, and the challenge of the parish to answer the needs of the neighborhood.

Upon receiving his letter of appointment, Charlie wrote to Archbishop Mitty thanking him, but also suggesting that Mitty might consider sending him to Hayward in Southern Alameda County so that Charlie's fluency in Portuguese might benefit that community. Luckily for Oakland, Mitty didn't follow his suggestion. While he continued his rural life activities in West Oakland, Charlie threw himself into a whirlwind of activities and projects which stressed the needs and issues of his parishioners. Even in the post-Depression days, West Oakland reflected its original grandeur with its rows of large wooden two-story Victorian faced duplexes. An outside staircase led up to two front doors which admitted one to a large downstairs flat and the other to a straight case to an upstairs apartment.

The advent of World War II and the birth of war industries changed the texture of the West Oakland neighborhoods dramatically, especially with the establishment of the Henry J. Kaiser shipyards in the Bay Area. Blacks and Mexican Americans poured out of the South and Southwest for wartime jobs. Oakland's Black population grew from 8,462 in 1940 to 32,327 in 1945. The low rent neighborhoods of West Oakland absorbed many of these new arrivals. Temporary housing projects, Campbell Village and Peralta Village, consisting of 550 units were constructed to meet the influx. The incoming Blacks were perceived by the dominant white population as a disruptive element who did not know their place. The weekly newspaper Observer in an editorial of March 11, 1944, reflected the general attitude of Whites toward Blacks. "The White man has the right to race prejudice if he so desires. If he cares not to associate with anyone, he is not compelled to do so. Right there is where the Negro is making a big mistake. He is butting into white civilization instead of staying in the perfectly orderly and convenient Negro civilization of Oakland and getting himself thoroughly disliked". It was perfectly acceptable to Whites to have the black Pullman porters and their families remain hidden in their deep West Oakland neighborhoods, but now Southern Blacks were appearing uptown, eating in restaurants, and shopping in department stores.

The Holy Names Sisters had educated hundreds of West Oakland children since 1886. They first lived in the convent house on 8th Street and in later years returned to Holy Names College on Lake Merrit. Since they did not drive automobiles, they depended on the priests for transportation. Sister Eileen Cronin, a former St. Mary's School principal, commented that "the sisters read many books waiting for the priests to drive them home." One day, Charlie transported them in an old black Model A Ford with balloon tires that he had picked up. The four door sedan sat very high, with the nuns in habits crammed inside. They pleaded with Charlie to take them home by side streets so that nobody would see them, but Charlie proceeded right up Broadway in full view of everyone with Charlie remarking, "Where's your holy vow of poverty?" During another trip the nuns were discussing the new I.Q. tests which they were giving to the students. Overhearing them he said, "You make me laugh at your I.Q. tests. Do you know what my I.Q. was when I was a kid? The seat of my pants!"

Charlie maintained a happy relationship with the Holy Names Sisters during his St. Mary's days with the exception of a $30,000 tax levied on St. Mary's and other East Bay parishes by the Archdiocese to construct a central Catholic girls' high school in 1932. The Archbishop's office had diverted $15,000 of St. Mary's parish funds on reserve in the Chancery Office and required the former pastor Father O'Connell to borrow another $15,000 from the Bank of America. Charlie's letter to Mother Redempta, the Holy Names Sisters Provincial, described the negative financial condition of the parish and school. The monthly income of the parish was not meeting expenses and the annual school deficits were due to the $30,000 debt for the high school.

These assessments levied against East Bay parishes were also loans which the Sisters were expected to repay. Charlie told Archbishop Mitty that nothing had been paid on the principal or the interest in eleven years. Likewise, only five St. Mary's girls were attending the high school, while a recent parish census conducted by the newly arrived Sisters of Social Service uncovered 243 children who had never received any religious education. Charlie's letter also pointed out that the Holy Names Sisters owned 1500 acres near Hayward which they leased out to tenants. "From the point of view of rural life, we are helping to establish feudal holdings and absentee landlords." Despite all of the criticism of his financial problems with the nuns, Charlie closed his letter by saying that he would be satisfied with the Sisters paying off sizable installments on the principal and in the spirit of early Catholic teaching omit the interest.

St. Mary's School attendance was dwindling so rapidly in 1937 that Charlie realized that he would not have enough students to survive. So with the Archbishop's permission, he made the school tuition-free. Eighty-five percent of the students lived outside the parish boundaries, which created a problem of control. The presence of St. Joseph's Church eight blocks from St. Mary's had been established as a National Church to serve the Portuguese population of the East Bay.

However, the Portuguese had long since departed West Oakland for neighborhoods in Hayward and San Leandro so that St. Joseph's was assigned to serve the newly arrived Mexican immigrant community. A large number of St. Mary's School students were Mexican whose parents attended St. Joseph's. Consequently, Charlie felt frustrated in providing free tuition on one hand and not having any control over these children. He discovered that the priests of St. Joseph's who were members of the Salesian Order insisted that the children of their families attend St. Joseph's, while the expectations of the school children were that they were to attend the 9 a.m. Mass at St. Mary's at which the school nuns would also attend and check on the children's attendance. So, Charlie faced the pressure of his school faculty and the force of the Salesian fathers down the street on the children.

Ron Dobbins of Piedmont, California, was a student at St. Mary's from 1930 to 1938. He fondly remembered Father Philipps' visit to the school every November 4th, the saint's day of his patron saint Charles Borromeo. The students knew that November 4th was a sure thing for a holiday but had to pretend that was like any other school day. Charlie would appear about mid-morning and make the announcement to the shouts and cries of the children. "To this day," remarked Robbins, "I always remember November 4th for Father Philipps."

The political arguments and differences between the two churches continued to the 1950's. In the late 1940's Charlie had two very active Spanish speaking assistant priests, John Duggan, whom Charlie sent to live in Mexico to learn Spanish, and Luis Almendares from Nicaragua. Almendares dedicated himself to the more educated and cultured Mexican, organizing a Guadalupe Society, a Young Peoples Club, choir, Spanish classes to improve their native language, and a library of Spanish books. Almendares was also a spellbinding orator who attracted Spanish speaking Catholics from all over the Bay Area. He also conducted a religious radio program. Duggan dedicated himself to poor families, the City and County jails, the general skid row population, and 'at risk' young males. He formed all kinds of sports teams, football, baseball, and basketball which kept these kids very busy and out of trouble. With a team of volunteers, he personally dug out the basement of the school and converted it into a clubhouse, complete with a boxing ring. Herb Robles of Alameda, California, and a former member as a boy, refereed to this group as "Duggan's Kids". "I have no idea how many kids didn't have time for the neighborhood gangs, because they played ball or boxed for Duggan, but a lot of them made it."

Resulting from the cultural conflicts and misunderstandings between Charlie's successor, Irish born John Walsh and the active Mexicans, the whole Guadalupe Society sneaked out with the ornate banner of Our lady of Guadalupe and the library and established themselves with the Salesians' blessings at St. Joseph's. The group was upset at the sudden transfer of their mentor Almendares to San Francisco. Duggan had been assigned to the Spanish Mission band. In place of these two native speakers, the St. Mary's Mexican community inherited me with my very limited language ability. While my Spanish improved with time, it took a few years before the departed leadership could be persuaded to return. However, their original activities and organization never regained the enthusiasm of the Almendares' days.

During his rural life activities as a country priest and Rural Life Director, Charlie had advocated and supported Mexican farm workers. Now in the city he turned his attention to the growing Spanish speaking population of West Oakland where most of the urban Mexicans had settled. He organized a meeting on the "Mexican Question" at St. Mary's on October 30, 1942, which included himself, Father Joseph Mulkern, Director of Catholic Charities of the East Bay who also resided at St. Mary's, Sister Patricia of the Sisters of Social Service, now members of the parish staff, and a Mrs. Dora Erickson, an educated Mexican woman who served as the Chairperson of the Pan–American Section of the National Council of Catholic Women of the Archdiocese of San Francisco.

Mrs. Erickson had been working very closely with the Social Service Sisters in the neighborhood. A census revealed the presence of over 250 Mexican families, most of whom were poorly educated in the religion, did not send their children to religion classes, did not attend Sunday services, and were being influenced by several Spanish speaking store front evangelical missions. Father Mulkern's report of the meeting stated that "unless something is done there will be the loss of numerous Mexican families to the Church." The group recommended that a Mexican priest be recruited to serve the Mexican community of West Oakland, establish store front centers and a settlement house with trained group work Spanish speaking staff to work with families in a variety of services. Another concern of the committee was the lack of English ability of Mexican students. The result of the meeting and report to the Archbishop was that none of these recommendations was implemented. The two churches of St. Mary's and St. Joseph's continued on their separate ways. People stayed within their own boundaries and served the community as best they knew how. Father Mulkern and Charlie became very close personal friends. Mulkern died at St. Mary's, and Charlie established a short lived boys' trade school there in Mulkern's memory.

Charlie had been aware of how ill-equipped the Church was in working with this increasing flux of Mexican immigrants. He had written to Archbishop Mitty about the multi-linguistic ability of European clergy, the bilingual ability of Southwestern priests to speak Spanish, "but only Menlo Park (the Major Seminary of the Archdiocese, St. Patrick's) sends out its men unfinished along that line. Spanish should be considered as a part of that training." Seminarian students at St. Patrick's became aware of the need long before Church authorities and began their own program of self–help groups taught by a few Spanish speaking students called "walkie talkie" classes conducted walking after the evening meals. Not until the late 1950's did the Archdiocese introduce a class called "Pastoral Spanish" at St. Patrick's.

Sister Eileen Marie Cronin taught at St. Mary's School three different times. She remembered Father Philipps as "very strict, compassionate, pastoral, kind, fatherly, and a warrior. He liked order and things done his way." She remembered him frequently out in the school yard with the children. Most of the students were poor Mexican kids who came to school very early in the morning because they had no heat at home. Charlie instructed Eileen Marie to make sure that every child receive a free breakfast before school, saying, "You can't teach these kids unless they have a full stomach."

Eileen Marie also remembered how Charlie liked to embarrass the nuns in public. Once, she asked him to accompany her and another sister companion to a lumber yard to buy paneling for the school library. After purchasing the material, Charlie remarked to the salesperson, " You know, you don't realize how lucky you are." "How is that?" inquired the man. Charlie responded "because you probably have only one wife, while I have two!"

The Holy Names Sisters by this time had established schools in Oakland, San Francisco, and Los Angeles. "There was a spirit at St. Mary's School," remarked Sister Eileen Marie," that I have never seen in any of our other schools." Among the community of Holy Names Sisters there was a saying that "If you can teach at St. Mary's, you can teach anywhere." The Holy Names Sisters had provided a quality education since 1886 to hundreds of West Oakland children of varied ethnic cultures and languages. They probably began with first generation Irish children and then worked their way through Greek, Portuguese, and Italian. Probably none of their schools reflected the varied ethnic mix of St. Mary's. Their final years were dedicated to immigrant, first language Mexican students who entered first grade speaking only Spanish.

That they succeeded so well with their students is a testimony of their skills and devotion. Father Antonio (Tony) Valdivia, now a Pastor in the Diocese of Oakland, California, recalled the influence of Father Philipps, the Holy Names Sisters, and the Social Service nuns on these Spanish speaking children. "There was no doubt that Father Philipps was not the boss at St. Mary's. He was El Senor Cura; elegant, direct, and forceful. If he didn't like your behavior, he'd pull you up by the sideburns. He was a wise man who realized that we were first generation Mexican Americans living in West Oakland. Most of our parents were Mexican immigrants. He wanted us to excel and be somebody. When he passed out report cards, he minced no words if you were doing poorly. We students were in awe of his language ability. We'd ask him to say something in French, then repeat it in German, Portuguese, and Spanish. Father Philipps never made us feel inferior, nor stopped us from speaking Spanish on the school yard, like what happened in other schools. He also gave us the idea that we had to make our religion a part of our lives, otherwise it was false."

Father Tony remarked that his family was not a church-going one when he was young. "As a third grader, my brother, sister, and I attended a summer Bible school conducted by Sister Patricia and the other Social Service Sisters. One day Father Philipps saw us in the school yard and suggested we ask our parents to send us to the parish elementary school. In those days, families paid one tuition, no matter how many children there were in the family. We had magnificent teachers in the Holy Names Sisters who were also big hearted. The majority of the students were Mexican who spoke English at school and Spanish at home out of deference to our elders. All of us second language learners needed special help in reading and spelling. Principal Sister Eileen Marie Cronin who founded the well known Raskob Learning Center at Holy Names College originated her famous theories and learning strategies with us at St. Mary's. Looking back at my classmates I can say that we all succeeded as Catholic priests, a Superintendent of Schools, several lawyers and teachers. Sister Mary Guadalupe from Mexico and raised in Los Angeles was not only our Principal but also the role model, mentor, family counselor to many Mexican women."

Father Tony recalled that his impression of the two churches was that St. Mary's was the "American" church while St. Joseph's took care of Italian, Portuguese, and Mexicans. "Both Father Duggan and Father Almendares brought distinct religious and social services to the neighborhood. Duggan dedicated himself to Mexican youth who were getting into Pachuco gangs. My mother credits him with saving my brother, John. Duggan was also a visionary. Culturally we were all in awe of our clergy and did whatever they suggested. Duggan once called a meeting of adults and young people to elicit our ideas and thoughts which was a whole new experience for us. He wanted to empower us and develop lay leadership. He was way ahead of the later lay movements in the church. I don't know why but I always remember that meeting. Father Almendares was good for people like my parents. He organized the Guadalupe Society, a choir, and had a spell binding presence as a speaker. People would not miss going to mass to hear him".

"Sunshine Camp, for us kids, was an outing and a half. Just to be up there in the country was an unforgettable experience. The seminarian counselors were fantastic people. They joked, were good athletes, and took very good care of us. They were also men of prayer to whom we could talk and share things we could not mention to our parents. I am sure that the seeds of my priesthood vocation were planted at Sunshine Camp. Father Philipps would cook pancakes for us on Saturdays. He really wanted to feed us and there was no lack of food. Later, when I returned as a counselor, I noticed that the children were a lot poorer than we were.

"The Salesian Fathers also conducted a minor seminary in Richmond, California, which started at the 8th grade level. I had the impression that the Diocesan parish clergy was meant for the Irish and not for us Mexicans. When Father Almendares heard that I had signed up with the Salesians, he barged through our front door yelling my mother's name. 'Cruz! What's this about Tony going to the Salesians? Jamas! ("Never")' He told her that I had to go to St. Joseph's College in Mountain View, California, the minor seminary of the Archdiocese because there was a great need for Spanish speaking parish priests. Even Father Philipps asked me why I had signed up with the Salesians and encouraged me to finish the 8th grade at St. Mary's."

Bob Valva is one graduate of St. Mary's School and parish that had fond memories of Father Philipps and the influence of the parish on young people of his time. Born in West Oakland, he attended St. Mary's Elementary School and McClymonds High School. He also attended Sunshine Camp first as a camper and later as a counselor. West Oakland and St. Mary's were strong influences on his life. "All of us kids would go to the 9 a.m. Mass on Sundays and then walk across the street to Jefferson Park which was our playground. St. Mary's was amazing in what it offered young people from 14 to 18 years of age. The Social Service Sisters organized all kinds of activities for us, especially the teen age clubs of Bachelors for boys and Debs for girls." One of his friends, Martin Page, formed his own band which played at the dances at the upstairs St. Mary's hall. Page later became one of Hollywood's best known music arrangers and composers. Following World War II military service Bill and his brother Bob returned to West Oakland and joined their father in the family business, Valva Realty.

Valva's father had immigrated from Italy, and eventually he took over his real estate business at 7th and Market Streets. When most real estate firms fled the declining West Oakland neighborhoods with the freeway eliminating every building below 6th Street, the Valvas stayed and saw the potential in the sale, maintenance, management, and rentals of old properties. "During the war," commented Bill Valva, "a lot of Southern Blacks as well as Mexicans from Mexico and the Southwest converged on West Oakland to work in the shipyards. West Oakland had cheap housing. Three families would occupy one house and rotate the beds as they worked three shifts. Some people lived in basements."

The Valvas ended up controlling West Oakland real estate. "When nobody would make loans in West Oakland we would guarantee them. Loan companies were reluctant to make loans because they didn't understand the neighborhood and they couldn't appraise properties. We taught poor people how to obtain housing by buying a low priced house, building up their equity, and then selling them a bigger house. Valva's housing philosophy in poor neighborhoods is "If it's strong enough, it's good enough." The Valvas were hired by CalTrans, the California State Highway Authority, to appraise the West Oakland properties slated for demolition because of the future freeway. The Valvas helped residents to obtain a fair price for their homes and also to buy other houses outside of West Oakland. Bill Valva commented, "I have taken care of four generations of home buyers. We started with little guys. That's what we know. There you have it! Bob and Bill Valva, born and raised in West Oakland with a high school education, home from World War II, started in business, and have accomplished as much and more than some college graduates."

"I will never forget Father Philipps, who married my wife Lois and I in February 1950 at St. Mary's. The church was packed with very prominent people from all over the East Bay. Philipps had never seen so many well-to-do folk in his church. When the bride reached the altar, Philipps uttered, 'Hold it! I want to take up a collection. He then instructed the Best Man and the ushers to get the baskets and begin taking up the collection. I think it was the first wedding in history that had a collection and the first time that many of my friends had a basket placed in front of them. And they put in a lot of money. Philipps also requested that any food left over from the wedding reception could be brought to the parish house for the needy. His sermon was all about poor people." Valva described Lois as being "all shook up" over Charlie's behavior.

The World War II years were active ones at St. Mary's. Charlie organized his own USO servicemen's activities with young women, sponsoring socials and dances. He even provided socials for 35 Italian POW's billeted at Camp Knight in Oakland and put together a group of young Italian speaking women. The Italian Colonel and the USA Charge d'Affairs expressed their heartfelt thanks to Charlie for this touching outreach effort.

Another time, a Mexican Navy vessel sailed into Oakland and docked at the Oakland estuary a few blocks from St. Mary's. Hearing about this, Charlie gathered a group of young Spanish speaking young women together to host the crew and officers at a dinner dance at the parish hall. Naturally, the seamen were overjoyed at meeting a group of friendly Mexican women and were grateful for Charlie's hospitality.

Sometime in the 1940's the Catholic cemetery workers at St. Mary's Cemetery, Oakland, went out on strike with their fellow workers of other cemeteries of the Archdiocse. The majority of these workers were Irish–born immigrants who had worked for the Church for years. The strike brought Bishop Hugh Donohoe to mediate the strike and represent the Archbishop in the negotiations. Donohoe had been a long time friend of Charlie's and returned to St. Mary's for lunch. Charlie listened to Donohoe's wails and then responded, "Well, we all believe in paying a living family wage to our workers. Let's see what it might cost for a family to live. Our worker is probably a good Catholic, doesn't practice birth control, and has at least six children who all attend parochial schools with one of them studying for the priesthood." By the time Charlie had finished his litany, Donahoe crept out of the rectory very embarrassed. Monsignor James B. Flynn, a longtime friend of Charlie's, described Charlie's words as typical of his forcing you to see reality in the raw.

His health declining and his hearing growing worse, Charlie requested permission from Archbishop Mitty to retire and continue to reside at St. Mary's. However, he placed one condition on his retirement, which was that he would continue to receive his monthly salary directly from the Archbishop's office and not from the parish which was too poor to afford two pastors' salaries. This arrangement continued until the advent of the Wagner years when the Chancery Office informed Wagner that the parish would now be responsible for Charlie's salary. Philipps erupted in anger when he was informed of the change. He wrote and protested saying that if the Archbishop would not honor the original agreement, he would embarrass him by marching up to Oakland's most important cross streets, 14th and Broadway, and begin selling pencils.

As long as he maintained his frail health, Charlie was able to continue his rural life work for a few years until turning it over to Father Donald McDonnell. He still hustled for his beloved camp and visited old friends. He had experienced the once vibrant West Oakland neighborhood of the early 20's and returned to experience it in slow decline from 1938 to 1950. He could no longer maintain his energy on "borrowed blood" as he would say. He slipped into convalescence and finally death on July 18, 1958.

One of my favorite St. Mary's stories occurred years after I had left there. In fact, it happened about 40 years later when I visited my sister Loretta Caufield and her husband Joe who operated an office business supply store in downtown Oakland. Needing a haircut, I asked them about the nearest barber shop to which they directed me about four blocks away. I entered this small shop and had to wait for the barber to finish up on a customer. When I finally sat down, I noticed that he was a tall Mexican American in his 50's with a full head of white hair. I also noticed a small homemade tattoo cross in the cleft of his hand next to his thumb. This mark I recognized as a popular one sported by the "Pachucos" of the 40's. I asked him if he had ever belonged to a gang, and he replied that he had it to be "one of the guys". His family had immigrated from New Mexico during World War II. After some questioning by me, he said that he attended St. Mary's Church as a young man. I asked if he ever remembered a Father Duggan which he did not. "No," he replied. "My priest was a Father Cox. One of the other priests at St. Mary's refused to baptize our baby because we were not married in the Church. Father Cox told us to come back the following Sunday, and he would do it. I'll never forget him."

At this point I told him to stop cutting and come around to face me. "Who do you see?" said I. He lowered his comb and scissors, looked long at me, and then wide eyed and shocked exclaimed "Jesus Christ! It's you!" I couldn't pay for the haircut.

ST MARY'S of THE IMMACULATE CONCEPTION

EST. 1853

St. Mary's Parish
Oakland, California

REV. CHARLES PHILIPPS, PASTOR
1936-1950

Rev. Gerald F. Cox
Associate Pastor
1950-1955

FIGHT NIGHT AT ST. MARY'S

Duggan's Kids

SISTER EILEEN MARIE CRONIN SNJM

PRINCIPAL. ST. MARY'S ELEMENTARY SCHOOL

SUNSHINE CAMP

$\mathcal{S}$hortly after I arrived at St. Mary's, in July 1950, I looked out of a window of the rectory to see a huge cattle truck with ten foot sides parked in the middle of the school yard. Forty to fifty Black and Mexican boys crowded around the truck clutching bed rolls, paper shopping bags, and battered suitcases containing their clothes and sundries for the next two weeks. Soon, boys and adult seminary counselors boarded the truck which pulled out of West Oakland, crossed the Richmond - San Rafael bridge, headed north up Highway 101, passing San Rafael, Santa Rosa, and Sebastopol. Winding past apple orchards, berry farms, and fruit stands along the Graventstein highway, the truck finally reached Sunshine Camp at Mirabel Park near the Russian River. The trip certainly violated every vehicle safety principle with kids and adults propped up against the sideboards. Probably the only reason why they weren't stopped by the California Highway Patrol was that everyone was hidden from view, but not out of earshot as campers and counselors sang their way north. This pilgrimage would be repeated four times each summer. The driver and owner of the truck was a cattle rancher friend of Charlie's, whom he knew in Stockton.

Helen DelPriore Hoffman, now of Lafayette, California, remembered her early days as a Sunshine Camper. "Our family name was DelPriore and we lived at 544 Linden Avenue in West Oakland from 1940 to 1946. Our neighborhood was a poor one. My sister, Lucy, and I attended St. Mary's School from 1941 to 1944. We were so poor and with my father out of work, tuition was hard to come by and we struggled to pay the $3 a month. Father Philipps was in charge of Sunshine Camp and I remember how my mother pleaded with him to let me and my sister go and she would pay $1 a week. He let us go and from the time we boarded the big truck until the time we came home, I will never forget his compassion for the poor. My sister only went one year because they had an age limit of 12 and he said 'no' to me because I wiggled too much and after all the seminarians were going to become priests and he didn't want them tempted. To this day the priest calls me Temptation. The name of the priest was Father Rassmussen. The other seminarians were great. They taught us how to swim. We stood in line for ice cream treats and games. We had a campfire and they told us scary stories. There was always lots of food and we felt special. If it wasn't for Father Philipps, I would not have such good memories of my sheltered childhood."

According to Monsignor Jim Flynn, the origin of the camp began in the late Depression days when Charlie one morning noticed a group of Mexican pupils seated on a school yard bench while other youngsters were enthusiastically running around. Charlie directed his assistant Father Tom Farrell to go down and see why these kids were not playing. Tom returned to inform Charlie that they hadn't eaten any breakfast and were hungry. This incident impelled Charlie to instruct his school staff to start a free breakfast program. He also saw the ideal use of his small apple ranch near Forestville to get these children out of the city and into the country for two weeks of sun, clean air, and nourishing food. This was the same 9-acre property given to him by a French woman parishioner in Sebastopol by Charlie's assuming the mortgage. In the beginning, the ranch contained a large two-story farm house, some sheds, and a small apple orchard located near the small town of Forestville and the nearby Russian River.

When he decided to start his camp, Charlie reached out to many of his old friends for help: Elizabeth Spread of Oakland, his longtime personal secretary, Mary and Joe Monager of Santa Rosa, Peggy and Bernard Squires from his Sebastopol days, Ruth and Pete Sharp, Alice Revel, and other young women from Holy Names High School, and seminary students from St. Patrick's Seminary, Menlo Park. Alice and her brother lived with their widower father who managed the Hotel Washington on 12th and Washington Streets, Oakland. A fellow Alsatian, he and Charlie remained close friends. Alice became the head of the girls' counselors at the camp.

Early seminary counselors Tom Regan, Elwood Geary, Chet Thompson, Howie Rassmussen, Eugene Duggan, Ray Cahill, and John Dietz were on staff. Later seminarians included Jim Flynn, Frank and Tony Maurovich, Art Harrison, Kelly Canelo, Dan Sullivan, Joe Marini, Ralph Brennan, John and Ben Cummins, Bill and Tom Burns, Milt Eggerling, Bill Duggan, Phil Conway, Jack McCarthy, Bill O'Donnell, and others.

Originally, boy and girl campers were poor White and Mexican kids from the St. Mary's West Oakland neighborhood. Later, Charlie's friend Bishop Hugh Donohoe, then Pastor of St. Mary's Cathedral in San Francisco, sent poor Black kids from the Fillmore District. Camp schedules included double two-week sessions for girls and boys. Altogether, about 200 children attended every summer. One approached the camp up a short straight road that ended with a row of five wooded cabins with a flag pole in front. Each cabin accommodated 10 campers on metal bunks fashioned out of quarter inch pipe with a wire mesh spring and a thin mattress on the top. The two-story farm house to the right housed Charlie's room and other staff members'. In ensuing years, he would add a closed-in kitchen, eating area, an infirmary, and a chapel. The interior of the chapel was finished in knotty pine which was considered "scrap" by the lumber yards in those days yet later on became quite fashionable material. Later, Charlie would boast that "he was way ahead of his time in interior design." He would offer Mass in the chapel on Sundays if he was there or send one of his St. Mary's assistants from Oakland who did not relish the five hour round trip just to say one Mass at the camp. Charlie received permission from the Archbishop to allow Catholics summering and living in the area to attend Mass at the camp. He also dutifully sent the Sunday collection to the Pastor of Sebastopol within whose parish boundaries the camp was located. Charlie had other plans for the camp in off-season months – such as a retreat center for working men. He visualized the camp as a spiritual training center for lay people. Among his papers in the Archdiocesan archives located at St. Patrick's Seminary is a cordial letter to Archbishop Mitty with a key to the camp, inviting the Archbishop to use the camp any time he wanted. He also had his eye on an adjoining piece of property, which he saw for a future air strip, which would save him driving time.

The daily routine of the camp followed that of most summer camp activities: A wake-up bell in the morning, washing, bed-making, flag raising, and Pledge of Allegiance. Breakfast followed, with the campers initially seated on railroad ties for their table and seats. Every Monday morning, Charlie was the official pancake cook. Decked out in a white apron, tall chef's hat, and holding a long spatula in his hand. Following breakfast, the kids played cowboys and Indians in the orchard and walked through the adjacent hop fields. Lunch was followed by a walk to the Russian River beach for swimming and playing on the beach. Most of these kids had never seen a river or had never gone swimming. In the 35 years of the camp's history, only one child died from drowning. A nap followed swimming and then a walk to the nearby store with a dime for treats. A French bath cleaned them up for evening dinner, which was always a lively occasion. Campers would sing to the cooks, "Come Out, Come Out". The cooks would file out of the kitchen greeted by applause.

Mary Monager, from Santa Rosa, served as the head cook for over 20 years. One day, a little Mexican boy banged on the screen door of the kitchen and was greeted by Mary holding a long wooden spoon. "Hey, Mary," he said, "I wanna tell you. You make better frijoles than my mother." Later Mary would brag to the counselors, "Don't you guys think you're so good. I make good frijoles!" One other time, a boy pushed his way to the front of the food line, was grabbed by counselor Phil Murray, and told to get to the rear of the line. Tony Valdivia, a counselor from the same neighborhood as the kids, told Phil to leave the kid alone and later explained, "...that kid is from a family of 13 kids and, at home, by the time he gets to the table, there might not be any food left." Murray got a real lesson on cross-cultural understanding. One day, a young camper had to be driven to the doctor in Sebastopol. After examining him, the doctor said, "There's nothing wrong with this boy. He's not used to such rich food." Camp food was nourishing and wholesome.

Aside from the meat from Sebastopol and the bread delivery, Charlie would get a counselor like Bill O'Donnell to drive him around to his old Sebastopol farmer friends where he would beg chickens, eggs, fruit, and anything else he could "mooch", as he had done in the Depression days.

Charlie didn't like to drive himself, preferring to have a chauffeur with whom he could evaluate the social problems of the day, the foibles of the Catholic Church, and the inherent evils of Capitalism. Charlie liked O'Donnell because Bill enjoyed working with his hands and also would laugh at Charlie's jokes. Charlie considered human sweat almost as a sacramental sign of wholeness and holiness. One of his favorite questions to newly arriving seminary counselors was "...are you here to smile or to sweat?"

The evenings around the campfire were filled with songs, spooky stories, and jokes. Here the creativity of the counselors would blossom in skits, songs, and stories and be passed down like doctrinal traditions. One of the most popular was "Anne Bolyne" boomed out by Tom Regan. "In the Tower of London, large as life, the ghost of Anne Bolyne walks I declare, I declare." The young brown and black faces glinting in the flickering fire, didn't know anything about English history, but they would roar back night after night, "With her head tucked underneath her arm she roams the bloody tower, with her head tucked underneath her arm at the midnight hour." The group would also sing a song called "Roll on Camp Sunshine, Roll On. We're as happy as we can be when we're not on K.P." and another to Charlie: "Hurray for Father Philipps, Father Philipps, our Pastor so dear". Several songs were identified with particular counselors who were pressed to sing every night. Howie Rassmussen's was "The King of Cannibal Island". John (now Bishop John Cummins of Oakland) and brother Ben sang "The Eskimo Fight Song", Chet Thompson, "Ave Maria", and Bud Duggan, "The Rose of Tralee".

When the evening campfire was over, kids would return to their bunkhouses and get ready for bed. When they were safely asleep, counselors, cooks, and Charlie would retreat to the kitchen area or to the big house for evening séances with Charlie, who was convinced his personal mission was to challenge and form the social consciences of these future priests. The Seminary courses of studies at Menlo Park included classes in Social Ethics taught by Bishop Donohoe and later by Monsignor Joseph Munier who was labeled the "Big Push" because he announced upon his arrival that he was commissioned to give "a big push to social justice issues." Charlie had his own Socratic style of deliberately throwing out statements like "the success of Communism in Europe was the failure of the Catholic Church to fight for the peasantry." Some nights, lively arguments broke out with some counselor defenders of the Faith rushing to shield the Church form Charlie's attacks. He would also relate the various fights for social justice that he had been involved in: The development of farmer cooperatives, the 160-acre limitation in the Central Valley, migratory labor, the evil powers of banks in foreclosing on small farmers, the growing danger of large corporations with millions of acres, the Associate Farmers of America, the Chamber of Commerce, and any group who benefited the rich and oppressed the poor. One among some of his favorite sayings was: "The evil man, you know what he's going to do. The damn fool, you never know what he's going to do." Charlie didn't spare the Church in his criticisms. He spoke about "damned ecclesiasticism". Some of his barbs were directed at bishops who would not stand up publicly for social justice issues. "Some bishops", he remarked one time, "are like monkeys. The higher up they go, the more of their ass they show!" His evaluation of the parochial school system and of celibacy was that they should be abolished. "They have made a fetish out of celibacy."

During the Sixties, the famous Brazilian educator Paulo Freire wrote a book called The Pedagogy of the Oppressed. Friere originated a completely new methodology to teach literacy to Brazilian peasants called "concientización" or consciousness raising. A group of peasants would look at the word "justice" on a blackboard and for days would discuss all the underlying and relative implications of the word for themselves. They thus became literate by deeply and communally examining the "gut" issues of their lives. Concientización was adopted by the Latin American Church and resulted in the growth of Liberation Theology and Communidades de Base, small basic communities, which evaluated the condition of their lives in light of the Gospel. Charlie, in his unique

way, pre-dated these consciousness raising methods which affected the
social justice development of these future priests. As a result of his influence, there were so many priests who ended up in social service activities, walking picket lines and boycotting grapes and lettuce in support of Cesar Chavez and the Farm Workers Union, working in the War
on Poverty programs, joining anti-Vietnam War demonstrations, and
going to jail for various causes. Jim Flynn related that a group of priests
who worked in the Catholic Charities Organization of the San Francisco Archdiocese once gathered in his quarters at St. Peter's Church. The
subject of Sunshine Camp came up in discussion. Jim looked around
the room at the various county Directors of Charities: Tim O'Brien,
Phil Conway, Ned Baker, and Jack McCarthy, all former Sunshine counselors. "It was not just accidental that what happened at Sunshine Camp
ended up in Catholic Charities," recalled Flynn.

Bill O'Donnell, now deceased, was probably the most radical product of Charlie's "boot camp". As the Co-Pastor of St. Joseph The Worker
Church of Berkeley, California, he was arrested and jailed more than
fifty times in demonstrating for farm workers, anti-Vietnam activities,
nuclear power, and labor union issues. He also traveled several times to
El Salvador in defense of the rebels' cause as well as to Guatemala. He
flew to Korea to join in a demonstration for the unification of North
and South Korea. Early in his priestly career, he was actually put under
house arrest by the former Bishop of Oakland, Floyd Begin, for getting
involved in racial issues in the City of Oakland. "Charlie," O'Donnell
remarked, "was a very strong character and a great inspiration to me
because he had the courage to fight the power structures. He preached
the plight of the poor. His standards were so high and demanding that
I thought 'Oh my God, he's like Jesus!' How did he get that way? I would
like to be just like him." Bill remembered that Charlie liked to counsel
and give seminarians advice about the practical aspects of life. During
one of the girls' sessions, he said, "You all think these little girls are just
innocent little children, but when they 'viggle' their little asses, you'll
give them anything they want. They're smarter than all of you."

Monsignor John McCracken, Pastor of St. Anne's Church, Wal-
nut Creek, California, remarked that Charlie created a whole group

of priests like Bob Moran and Red Lenniger who later became community activists. So many former seminarians would say in later years that "Sunshine Camp" was the most valuable experience I ever had." Or, "Charlie was way ahead of his time in seminarian formation. He had his own internship program." Bill Cane, a Sunshine counselor and former active priest, now living in Watsonville, California, and working in community development projects, recalls 'Pop Philipps' in his book Circles of Hope. Cane came to know Pop in the 1950's following his retirement. He listed some of Charlie's famous remarks at his evening camp sessions: "When you are ordained, do not let your ecclesiastical ass become so wedded to your chair that it takes a $10 Mass offering down in the parish office to separate them." Also, "Don't be like the monks who meditate on the thirty-second degree of humanity, when they don't have the first degree." One Sunday in the Chapel he spoke at Mass, saying, "I don't talk about plaster saints. I am going to talk about the Sweeneys here in the front pew who have a large family. They come here, work, cook, build, and do dishes. Those are the kind of saints I will talk about." In his remembrances of Charlie, Cane "did not realize that Charlie was passing a living spirit on to him."

Father Chet Thompson, a former Sunshine Camp seminarian counselor, made a trip to the camp with his pious father to visit Charlie, the cooks, and other volunteers. Chet had just returned from the Catholic University of America after three years study of Canon Law, where he received his Doctorate. Chet proudly announced to Charlie, "Well, I made it!" Charlie who hated the legalisms of Canon law and Canon Lawyers responded, "Well, there goes another good man wasted!"

There were so many dramatic and humorous happenings at the camp over the years, but one of the most dramatic was related by Peggy Squires, the story of the old well which was not producing much water and needed to be deepened by Charlie's handyman, Lester, and some counselors. The day that the work was to begin, Charlie called Bernard Squires in Healdsburg at four o'clock in the morning and told him to drive over to the camp to tell Lester and all not to descend into the well. He explained that he had a dream in which all of the bricks lining the well fell to the bottom. Within twenty-four hours they did! Did he have a guardian angel, or was he also psychic?... perhaps both.

Although Charlie was the founder and president of the camp, he maintained a very democratic delegation style of management. He put Jim Flynn in charge and gave him a free hand as if to say, "Don't bother me with details." Jim's aunt Marie Walsh was Charlie's housekeeper at St. Mary's Church, and following the death of his parents in Portland, Jim came to live at St. Mary's and had a room there during his seminary days. Charlie became a surrogate father for Jim. Charlie could also display flashes of stubbornness and anger toward the counselors. Alice Ravel, one of Charlie's most dependable young women counselors, decided to enter the Holy Names Sisters novitiate following her high school graduation. Charlie had known Alice and her Alsatian father since going to Oakland. When Alice went to Charlie for a recommendation to enter the convent, "he balked and hesitated," remarked Alice, now Sister Louise Marie. He didn't want to give me a recommendation "because he knew that he would be losing his Chief Cook and Bottle Washer." Sister Louise also remembered another occasion when Pat Finnegan, one of the seminarian counselors, picked her up in his car after classes at Holy Names High School. One of the eagle-eyed nuns who knew Pat saw them and reported the incident to Charlie, who was also Alice's Pastor and Camp Director. Charlie waited until the camp opened before he approached Alice about this innocent incident, now overloaded with innuendo. One day he told Alice to get into his car with two other seminarian counselors. They drove out to camp for a few miles and then stopped the car. Charlie turned to Alice and shouted, "Why are you ruining a young man's vocation?" and proceeded to relate the story relayed to him by the high school nun. Alice was speechless and humiliated. Charlie never took back his accusations nor asked for her forgiveness. At the same time, he never spoke to Finnegan about ruining Alice's religious vocation.

The most hilarious tale that went down in Sunshine lore was the story about Charlie taking the camp cow to be bred. He had purchased the cow to show the campers exactly where and how you got milk by having them participate in the milking chores every day. When Charlie announced that he was going to a nearby ranch to service the cow with a friendly bull, the counselors and campers decided to make the event into a celebration. They decorated the cow and the trailer with bows, ribbons, and all kinds of decorations. They hooked the trailer up to the camp pickup and off went Charlie to the assembled "Hoorays" and words of encouragement from the assembled campers and counselors. Charlie, of course, assumed that the "heifer service" would be a gratuity because of the camp. He never liked to pay for anything, assuming that he was giving people any opportunity to demonstrate their generosity to his kids. He once entered a hardware store in Sebastopol and asked the young high school boy clerk the price of a wrench. When the young man replied "$2.35", Charlie answered – "It's only worth fifty cents! I'll give you fifty cents." The boy was very bewildered at what to say to this brusque elderly clergyman until the owner, who knew Charlie, yelled from the rear of the store, "Give it to Father Philipps for fifty cents!"

Several hours after Charlie's departure with the cow, the truck and trailer roared up the camp driveway, skidded to a stop, and out jumped Charlie slamming the truck door and with anger written all over his face yelling, "Fifty Dollars for one fuck! That's outrageous!" The cattle rancher wasn't as generous as Charlie thought he would be. That summer "Fifty Dollars for one fuck" became the popular motto whenever counselors wanted a laugh.

The spirit and atmosphere of Sunshine Camp was one of a loving and caring community of campers, cooks, and counselors. These Mexican and Black youngsters found big brothers and sisters in the volunteer mothers, in the women cooks, and God the Father in Charlie. During the school year, campers would travel to St. Patrick's Seminary on visiting Sunday, trade letters, and attend ordinations and First Masses. Sunshine created a very positive image of the Church for these kids who carried these memories into their adult lives. The imprint of a caring Church was one of Charlie's original purposes in founding the camps. In a November 11th, 1938, letter to Archbishop Mitty, Charlie wrote "My final end is to make them practical Catholics in later life when they will appreciate what Christ's Church did for them in their handicapped childhood. I always have Russia, Spain, and Mexico in mind."

Sunshine Camp had no budget, no grants, and no community charities, nor any official Church support. It must have had an Alsatian guardian angel to keep it going. No salaries or stipends were paid as everybody worked for free. Charlie was a one-man fund raising machine. As soon as the camp formally closed in September with an annual steak barbecue for benefactors and volunteers, Charlie was up, raising donations, and picking up any materials he would lay his hands on. He kept contact with some of his wealthy friends at St. Bridget's Church who were very generous to him. Archbishop Mitty often sent him personal donations. A Christmas appeal letter in December 1955 stated that the previous camp season had taken care of over 200 children. "How?" it asked. "A budget? What is that? Our way is 'foolishness to the Greeks' as St. Paul said. But it works! Three square meals plus a couple of snacks for everybody, thanks to the contributions of charitable groups, of kind persons, including some pastors and of so many young priests, former counselors. So whilst I do not know our rating on the Dow-Jones Index, no sheriff and no agent of the Better Business Bureau has ever paid a visit to the Camp. Simple Christian charity still works and prospers in the warm atmosphere of the God-Child in the crib." Charlie had a humorous quip for donors. "If your check doesn't have three figures, don't write it." A San Francisco donor who gave an annual gift of $1,000 once requested an audit of Camp finances before he would give the next year. Charlie's response was, "The hell with him." He never made a show of thanking people. He thanked them sometimes, almost curtly, because he believed he was actually offering them an opportunity to do something great.

One of the camp fundraisers that was offered to Charlie by Jimmy Dundee and Harold Broom, both prize fight promoters, was a benefit boxing event at the old Oakland Auditorium on Lake Merrit, the scene of many famous prize fights. Wednesday nights became "fight night" in Oakland beginning in the 1930's and continuing for the next several decades. Many neighborhoods vied with each other over which one produced the best boxers. Watts Tract had its Teddy O'Hara and West Oakland a large contingent including "Battling" Benny Vierra and Bobby Dalto who fought under the name of "Bobby Burns". The famous

Max Baer from Livermore, California, was a frequent fighter in Oakland in the early 1930's. His claim to fame was his winning the heavyweight championship with an 11th round knockout of Primo Carnero of Argentina in June 1934.

Oakland also sported a number of boxing gyms where fighters trained. Jimmy Duffy operated the best known one, "Duffy's" at 424 11th Street, directly across the street from the old T & D theatre, affectionately called the "Tough and Dirty". The well respected Harry Fine managed "Duffy's" gym. The Yosemite Athletic Club at 500 Union Street at 5th Street had Joe Ferreira as its manager and was frequented by boxers from West Oakland. Uptown, at 534 20th Street, Jimmy Duffy's old partner Harold Broom ran the Imperial Athletic Club. Broom, legally known as H. Algernon Broom, was regarded as the best fight trainer in the Bay Area. Dundee was a former featherweight boxer (1913-1922). He and Broom had been boyhood friends since 1902 when they sold newspapers together. They established The Ringside bar at 1011 Franklin Street in 1937 as a social club for fighters. Art Cohen, the renowned Sports Editor of the <u>Oakland Tribune</u> had a seat of honor at the bar and dubbed the place "The Poor Man's Stork Club". Broom once reported that "we never have any fights in this place. This is because we do not allow any unescorted women in this dump. Only wives and dames."

Broom and Dundee offered Charlie a benefit prize fight card for the support of Sunshine Camp with the main even featuring the popular local fighter "Bobo" Olsen, a top ranked middleweight at the time. Charlie had never witnessed a boxing match, and since he was the feature beneficiary, he had to make an appearance. So he pressed me into taking him to the Oakland Auditorium. The Wednesday night fight crowd was surprised to see two Roman Catholic priests walking down the aisle to the front row of seats of honor. Before the first card was announced, Charlie was introduced and Sunshine Camp mentioned as the recipient of the benefit. Charlie stood up and waved to the crowd who gave him a very loud applause. A ringside seat gives one a whole different view from someone in the 15th row. Up close you see the sweat fly off the fighters' faces, the blood spurting out of facial cuts, hear the head butts, and feel the body blows on the fighter pinned to the ropes in front of you. This view was not Charlie's cup of tea. He was fundamentally a very compassionate person, and this display of physical violence was too much for him. We had to stay for the main event, which lasted four rounds. Then, after thanking Broom and Dundee, we beat a quick retreat for home. I don't think Charlie repeated the benefit again.

Charlie celebrated his 70th birthday September 17th, 1951. A cartoon drawing of Charlie in the camp jeep shows him driving through the camp. Twenty-two signatures of seminarian counselors appeared on the drawing which declared "Any damned fool could live to be 70!" Charlie penned the following: "To make my foolish Sunshine Camp work, it takes all of you Fools of Christ as counselors. Fools of Christ of devoted cooks, and an Archfool of Christ to run it at 70." Five years later, he wrote to congratulate Archbishop Mitty on his Golden Jubilee and informed him that because of illness, he was unable to attend. He reminded Mitty that he had crossed the 75th milestone. His letter continued to describe his end of the year "Peasant Dinner" where he was able to thank "113 volunteers for their 19 years of dedicated service. Forty young priests, former counselors, were present, graduates of our practical training school for social services."

Monsignor John McCracken in, 1951, was the Assistant Director of Catholic Charities in the East Bay and was living in residence at St. Mary's Rectory. One night Charlie walked into his room and asked him, "John, how would you like to be a member of the Sunshine Camp Board of Directors?" McCracken answered that he already had too many commitments and suggested that Charlie recruit someone else. "Well, John," said Charlie, "I'm afraid it's too late for that. You were voted in on the Board tonight, in fact, you are also the Vice President." Following Charlie's death in 1957, McCracken assumed direction of the camp for the next fifteen years. He had previously asked Charlie what he would like to happen to the camp after he was gone. Charlie replied that he did not want it handed over to the Archdiocese. He preferred that it could maintain its original purpose of serving poor children. When McCracken informed the Archbishop that he was assuming direction of the camp, Mitty exclaimed, "You can't run that camp!" McCracken insisted that he could, and Mitty waived him aside muttering, "I think you're crazy." Elizabeth Spread, one of Charlie's closest friends and personal secretary, remained as the camp's secretary/treasurer. John called her in February to inquire what the camp check book balance was, and she replied, "Oh, about $500." McCracken panicked and exclaimed, "Elizabeth, you've got to be kidding! What are we going to do? We're supposed to open in middle of June!" "Don't worry, Father," she answered in her soft and sure voice, "the money will come in. It always does. When I start worrying, then you can start." That was the rule of thumb that McCracken followed afterwards. All of a sudden, check after check would arrive to cover the expenses that year. McCracken managed the camp until 1970 when he could no longer recruit seminarians who were being assigned to summer internships in local parishes. In the last year, a little girl drowned in the Russian River, dampening the enthusiasm and the spontaneity of the camp. A top Sonoma County Appraiser was engaged to get a value on the property, which was sold to neighbors for $120,000. The Sonoma County Appraiser's office called McCracken to ask why he sold so cheaply. "Because I couldn't pay the taxes", he replied. The proceeds of the sale were divided equally and given to the San Francisco, Oakland, and Santa Rosa Catholic Dioceses to provide summer camperships for poor children.

Charlie's Peasant Farm finally came to an end. No more fire bell broke the morning stillness to tumble the campers out of bed, small brown and black bodies were no longer splashing in the nearby Russian River, the strains of Anne Bolyne had departed from the evening air, the Monday morning pancake Bishop had laid down his spatula. Charlie's dream of bringing poor children out of the atmosphere of the ghetto had gone on for 35 years. Over 4,500 inner city kids for the first time in their lives picked an apple off a tree, pulled tomatoes off a bush, milked a cow, swam in the Russian River, ran in the waves of the Pacific Ocean at Jenner by The Sea, ate three full meals, sang campfire songs, and loved and were loved by a group of caring adults, especially the old man with the red neckerchief who started the whole thing.

Any damned fool could live to be 70!

Sunshine Canyon 1957

a truth, flattering in its disrespectfulness

Charlie and Kids

"Down By The Riverside"

Seminarian Counselors and Camp Staff

SISTERS OF SOCIAL SERVICE

⸰⸱◯⸱⸰

*P*eggy Squires, Charlie's longtime friend from Sebastopol, once commentated that "when Father Philipps was in Sebastopol, he was all for the farmers, but when he went to Oakland, he dedicated himself to poor children." Although he had himself as Pastor, two assistant priests, and an elementary school staffed by the Holy Names Sisters, he realized that he needed an outreach component of religious women to work in the neighborhood, visit families, conduct children's education programs, and organize a comprehensive social services program. Hearing about the Social Service Sisters in Los Angeles, he immediately contacted the Superior, Sister Frederika Horvath, who made an informal visit to St. Mary's in late 1937. Charlie arranged a meeting on March 5, 1938, with the Chancery Office official Monsignor J.M. Byrne, Secretary to Archbishop Mitty, and Sisters Fredeika and Sister Lucille of Sacramento, where the sisters had a mission. Byrne's report of the meeting to the Archbishop had a humorous introduction by describing the sisters' dress. "Outfitted in a gray habit, modest but not of usual style of religious, same habit, except hat, was used inside of the convent." Had he had more acquaintance with women's fashions, his report could have read: "Archbishop, you won't believe it! I went into this room to meet two nuns who looked exactly like Red Cross ladies, long gray skirts, long gray sleeved blouses, gray hose, black shoes, and a gray pillbox hat with a gray short veil. Suspended around their necks they wore a long silver chain, which held a large silver medallion of the Holy Spirit, the group's special patron."

The sisters displayed a definite interest in an Oakland mission, described the nature of their social service apostolate, and suggested that Charlie outline a list of activities which could be translated into a contract between the Archbishop, Father Philipps, and the Sisters. They concluded the meeting saying that their earliest arrival date in Oakland could be Pentecost of 1939. Charlie wrote to the Archbishop on September 1, 1939, thanking him for the courteous and cordial reception he gave them the previous week. "It is my intention from the beginning," he wrote, "to use the Sisters as a foundation around which to rally and train Catholic leaders in the different social activities of the day."

He outlined a list of programs and activities, which were developed into a contract. Two Social Sisters would staff the service activities of St. Mary's Parish and provide general social services to parish families and settlement house programs of clubs and organizations for children and young adults and organize religious education classes and other related activities. The parish would furnish the Sisters with the former convent of the Holy Names Sisters, a salary of fifty dollars per month per sister, an automobile, and an annual four weeks vacation plus ten days for a religious retreat.

Charlie and the Sisters of Social Service were made for each other. Both were committed to the service of the poor and the development of lay leadership. The Sisters owed their origins to a group of progressive women who in 1908 established the "Social Missions Society" for the purpose of developing professionally trained women social workers Their first project served young women offenders on probation and young ladies who came to the city to work. Dedicated to the Holy Spirit from the beginning, the pioneer nuns adopted "Sisters of Social Service" as their official name on May 12, 1923, with Sister Margaret Slacta as the foundress of the new Sisters of Social Service. The goal of the group was to train women as social workers and serve whatever community social problems might exist, especially those affecting women, children, and families.

Headquartered in Budapest, the Sisters developed leadership training courses for female members of trade unions, started needle craft, printing, and cottage industry cooperatives operated by women, a school of agriculture and home economics, and conducted retreats for lay people, They also became consultants and trainers of women's and young girls' organizations engaged in social welfare work. One of their members, Sister Margaret Slacta organized a national women's political party, the Christian Women's Party whose purpose was to work for the welfare of women, children, and families. Eventually the Christian Women's Party grew to include the whole country of Hungary.

The Sisters were original community organizers of women's political power, traveling throughout Hungary and awakening women to the necessity of uniting themselves. Sister Margaret became a strong voice for economic and social reforms in Hungary. Following World War II, the Sisters also founded a newspaper for the working women's movement entitled "The Young Christian Working Woman". In recognition of her work, Sister Margaret was elected to a seat in Parliament, the first woman in Hungary to receive this honor, which opened the political doors in Hungary for other women to participate and contribute to Hungarian society.

As soon as Charlie announced the arrival of the Social Sisters from the pulpit and in newspaper releases, all kinds of volunteers contacted him, expressing their desire to participate: Public school teachers for English and citizenship classes, four young lawyers to provide legal aid, and a Dental Hygienist from the University of California Medical Center, San Francisco, as well as two women social workers. Charlie also mentioned that he had received encouragement to begin a volunteer nurse service. Charlie's friend from his previous parish in Pinole, Miss Dorothy Galt, a Senior Dental Hygienist at University of California Hospital, San Francisco, was placed at St. Mary's School one afternoon per week during the Spring semester. She examined all of the students' teeth and discovered that every one of them needed urgent dental attention. Parents were notified, twenty-six students were referred for immediate care, six children's teeth were cleaned, and fifteen classroom classes on dental care and nutrition were conducted.

Charlie made serious plans to involve the Sisters in operating a residence for unemployed single women. Over a period of six years from 1944-1950, the Sisters housed a number of young women at the convent, two of whom had left religious novitiates and were trying to adjust to living in society. The plans were to have the Sisters operate an eight to ten room house during the day with a woman volunteer and a night housemother. Charlie interested and invited a number of Oakland influential women to become involved. Ms. Dora Erickson, Ms. Emmett McCoy, and Ms. Harry Howard organized a Board of Directors, but sadly Charlie had to abandon his dream for lack of financial support for the project. He wrote to Archbishop Mitty that he could not realize his original hopes.

The original corps of sisters consisted of Sister Vincentia, Superior, Sister Miriam, and Sister Florence. The convent at 8th and Jefferson Streets consisted of a two story brown shingled building that was connected to a library, conference room, and social center where programs were held. The first one, after a neighborhood needs assessment was made, was the investiture of a Catholic Girl Scout program with organizational training provided by the Oakland Girl Scout Council. The two troops were the beginning of Catholic Girl Scouts in the city of Oakland. Other services and projects developed a Filipino "Family Group" to promote the religious, cultural, and civic welfare of many East Bay Filipinos; a Business Women's Club with commercial arts training for young women over 18; a first summer vacation school with four weeks of Bible study, singing, and handicrafts for neighborhood children who did not attend the parish school, and for those socially disadvantaged, especially children from large Mexican families whose fathers worked for the Southern Pacific Railroad Company.

While these sisters laid the foundation and the spirit of their parish mission, it was Sister Patricia Feely who developed the Settlement House services for the next 25 years. Born in St. Paul, Minnesota, December 8, 1904, she was the only girl and sister in a family of 10 brothers. Her Irish immigrant parents operated a creamery. Her mother died when she was 8 years old, leaving her to be raised by her father and ten brothers. She grew up to be a free spirit. As a young woman she came West to San Francisco and was inspired to join the Sisters of Social Service in

Los Angeles by a Jesuit priest cousin, Father Raymond Feely, S.J. of the University of San Francisco. Patricia made her religious profession on September 24, 1936, and was assigned to a mission in downtown Sacramento where she first conducted a census in a neighborhood which included the red light district. She arrived at St. Mary's as Superior with a Sister Magdalene in 1940 where she developed and expanded services until 1965.

Sister Patricia was an unusual person with the ability to discover leadership, to initiate and sustain programs for neighborhood people and families. Mrs. Dora Grace Erickson, a native Mexican and Professor of Spanish at Holy Names College, collaborated with Sister Patricia in developing programs and services for the growing Mexican community of West Oakland. The first Spanish newspaper was born at St. Mary's Center, as well as the first celebration in Oakland of Las Posadas, the traditional Mexican Christmas celebration. World War II and the large influx of military personnel in the Bay Area inspired Sister Patricia to develop St. Mary's Center as a drop-in facility for servicemen and young women away from home. She also recruited seminarians who had been counselors at Sunshine Camp as volunteers for her summer school programs and her annual Christmas party at the Center, which drew some 400 children for a variety show and treats.

Sister Patricia also had a genius for inspiring the hidden talents of young sisters, lay volunteers, and seminarians, many of whom credited her for sustaining their religious commitment. Over the years she became a mentor and example for young sisters, allowing their talents to develop as well as sharing her humor and free spirit. One young woman, Julie Durack from Detroit, became a volunteer and delivered food to poor families living in nearby wartime housing sites. Julie eventually left Oakland, joined the Maryknoll Sisters, and worked as a missionary in Korea where she is buried.

The end of World War II witnessed widespread unemployment and unrest, with people knocking on the convent door for help. Sister Patricia was joined at this time by a Sister Benedict who helped create the St. Mary's Soup Kitchen where every morning homeless men and women lined up for the only meal they might get that day. The famous Dorothy

Day of the Catholic Worker Movement visited the Sisters during this period and complimented them on their service to the homeless. The Soup Kitchen was the foundation of the St. Vincent de Paul kitchen in downtown Oakland many years later. Following the death of Father Philipps, the Sisters realized that they could not live and work in the same location. They were burning out with the constant knocks on the door and pleas for help. They needed a place where they could recharge and then return to continue their work. A large house was purchased on Trestle Glenn Road in the Lakeshore District of Oakland through the efforts of a Woman's Guild formed in 1954, and the house was paid off after 10 years.

Sister Patricia also established a house in Santa Clara and worked there from 1962 to 1969 when she returned to Oakland. Shortly afterwards, she contracted breast cancer as well as struggled with heart and breathing problems. She was spared the fear of a long lingering illness by falling down the back stairs of the Sisters' residence and breaking her neck. She died at Providence Hospital on August 17, 1972. Her spirit and devotion to the poor lived on in the many young sisters and lay leaders whom she inspired.

Sister Rosanne Curtiss was another member of the St. Mary's community. She arrived with Sister Rita Anne Weitekamp to join Sister Patricia and worked in West Oakland for 11 years. Rosanne joined the Social Service Sisters after working as a secretary at Catholic Social Services, San Francisco, getting married, and shortly afterwards, becoming a World War II widow with the death of her G.I. husband in the Pacific. Through her participation in the Young Christian Workers Movement at St. Boniface Church, San Francisco, she was attracted to the social service dimension which the Social Service Sisters offered.

She remembered the wonderful feeling of community at St. Mary's where the Sisters directed social clubs for young Filipinos and Latinos, operated the soup kitchen for 50 homeless men every day and a free clothing center for families, conducted a neighborhood census, recruited children for religious instruction, and signed up campers for the annual trek to Sunshine Camp. "Most of the families in the neighborhood were the working poor with large numbers, " she remarked. "Very few were welfare recipients." Remembering Father Philipps, she recalled, "Some people called him a Communist but I think he was more of a Socialist. He exhibited the spirit of the Vatican Council long before the Council happened. He always said The Bishops should be with the people. She also recalled the number of young adults formerly active at St. Mary's who returned as volunteers: the Valva brothers, Bill and Bob, who remained in West Oakland and served the neighborhood through their real estate business, and Ray Dami and his wife who operated a pharmacy at 8th and Washington Streets and who gave the sisters free medications for the poor, represented the quality and generosity of the many volunteers who lived Christ's message to tend to the poor. We lived in the West Oakland community and worked hard. We attended Sunday mass at the parish church in order to meet the parishioners and make contacts. I think I did more good in those days than what I am doing now as Director of Catholic Social Service in Vallejo. We were really with the poor and part of their community. One of our Sisters who had received her Master's Degree in Social Work once remarked that at St. Mary's we were doing 'old fashioned' stuff. The whole field of Social Work had gone in the direction of clinical therapy in an attempt to solve human problems. Our kind of supportive therapy had fallen out of style. But we have returned to feeding the poor, getting them jobs, and housing."

The twenty-plus years of service by the Social Service Sisters came to a sad and comical ending in 1969 after Sister Cecelia had received free tickets to an evening performance of the Ice Follies in San Francisco. Sister Cecelia, some women volunteers, and fifteen girls took off in three old autos, one of which broke down on the way home. Some worried mothers called the then current Pastor, Father Joseph Pier at 1 a.m. looking for their daughters. Pier assured the mothers that the Sisters wouldn't be out so late at night. Later, when he discovered that indeed they had been out late, he became furious and reported the incident to Sister Fredericka, the Provincial Superior in Los Angeles, describing the "Follies" as some kind of a bawdy vaudeville show rather than an ice skating performance. As a result of this incident, Sister Fredeika sent a directive to all of their convents, forbidding any presence at future "Follies".

This incident led to the death of any working relationships with Father Pier and the Social Service Sisters, who pulled out of St. Mary's shortly afterwards. Philipps' vision of creating lay leaders and meeting the needs of West Oakland's poor were realized through the 25 years of mission by the Sisters of Social Service. If a Poor Peoples Hall of Fame were ever instituted in West Oakland, one would see the following women who left their mark at St. Mary's: Sisters Vicentia, Miriam, Florence, Patricia, Rosanne, Rita Anne, Martina, Benedicta, Johanna, and Cecelia. The spirit of their foundress Margaret Slacta lived on in their love and dedication to women, children, and families. Originally they were a new kind of "nun", comfortable in modern dress and at home walking the streets of the poor, and became in Oakland the embodiment of Charlie Philipps' belief in living in service to the needy. Their presence at St. Mary's personalized that famous quote of Cardinal Emanuel Suhard of Paris, France, "One cannot be a saint and live the gospel we preach without spending oneself to provide everyone with the housing, employment, goods, leisure, education etc., without which life is no longer useful."

Sister Patricia/ Morning Bread Line

In line with his unabated zeal for
renewing Christian principles in society and particularly among his own
parishoners, in 1939, Father Philipps
opened Saint Mary's Social Center.
Devoted to religious, social and recreational activities, it became a
home to the Order of the Sisters of
Social Service who had been called to
the parish that year. The Order had
been founded in Los Angeles in 1926.
Arriving to serve the needs of the
community were Sister Bernardine,
Sister Miriam, Sister Florence, Sister Lucile, Sister Vincentia (Superior), who formed the foundation of the
settlement house.(Photo, Saint Mary's.)

CATHOLIC RURAL LIFE

❧⊙❧

*C*harlie's activities as the Catholic Rural Life Director began in Sebastopol in 1933 and continued until 1952, following his retirement in 1950. His "Apologia Pro Vita Mea" was very clearly and seriously stated in one of his many appearances before agricultural hearings and meetings. On March 1st, 1945, he read a statement before a California State Chamber of Commerce Meeting where he said, "Gentlemen, I speak here as a member of the most conservative body in the world, the Roman Catholic Church. I have been considered a radical and my radicalism comes from the fact that I have a general, personal and genuine outlook on farming diametrically opposed to the general view." He then described his background as the son of Alsatian peasant parents who successfully raised six children, two of whom were university graduates. "I make bold to declare that, like my father, I am a successful man, speaking six languages with some Latin and Greek on the side." He made a strong plea that banks and lending institutions ought to finance returning service men without interest because of their contribution to the community. "You speak of fertilizer and I speak of manure. You speak in terms of the sacred two and four percent and the amortization of principal to be saddled on G.I. Joe. Bear in mind that our returning servicemen back from the far flung battlefields will not stand for your taking his shirt away in the form of interest and principal for forty years."

His philosophy was also inspired and shaped by the Church's social justice teachings, especially the Papal Encyclicals, which he frequently quoted. He also saw the potential of the Church to work for and speak out for the "country", particularly the small farmer, ranch, or dairyman, although he was realistic enough to know that the Church's priorities lay in urban areas. In his April 7th, 1933, Easter letter to St. Sebastian parishioners, he stated that upon arriving in Sebastopol, he "was moved to take a personal and direct interest in the farmer's lot. I do not pretend to solve the more pressing problems of today, primarily I am interested in the moral principles, the moral values which should form the background of our national and local conditions." The letter then proceeds with a long list of quotes from Pope Leo XIII's 1891 Encyclical on Capital and Labor and Pope Pius XII's Reconstruction of The Social Order on the rights of workers, legislation of social justice, and oppression of working men. Charlie referred to the encyclicals as the "radical declarations of the Pope."

In a long letter to Monsignor Luigi G. Ligutti, National Director of the National Catholic Rural Life Conference, in Des Moines, Iowa, Charlie stated that he wished to convey his personal viewpoint and convictions about the role of the Church's rural life program. "It seems to me that our Rural Life setup, philosophy, and the actual carrying out of plans is an outstanding, practical achievement of the church in America." He lamented the fact that priests with rural life experiences who became bishops would be influenced by other urban-minded bishops. "They surround themselves with canonists (Church Canon Lawyers) in order that they may always proceed with prudence and safety. They are naturally conservative and play to the so-called conservative element." Charlie goes on to blast an article in the Catholic press by a Bishop Schlarman who criticized the Mexican government for breaking up large haciendas because the peasants did not produce as much as the hacendados. "What stand," he asked, "did the Hierarchy of California and the United States take in regard to the elimination of the 160-acre limitation in Federal Reclamation projects? Not a peep!" Charlie ended his message to Liguitti by saying that if the National Conference cannot convince the Bishops to support the small family farmer, "then our Rural Life, which has in itself so much vitality and so much power for revolutionizing the thinking of our Bishops and the thinking or our

Catholic press and literature, will be remembered as sweet poetry and wishful utopia."

Liguitti and Charlie became long time friends and correspondents. They both shared European peasant backgrounds, Charlie from Alsace-Lorraine and Liguitti from the small Italian village of Romans in the province of Udine. Charlie finished his education and priestly training in Europe while Liguitti emigrated to Des Moines, Iowa, with his family and attended American Seminaries. Both became rural pastors and involved themselves in the lives of the farmer families. Liguitti guided the national office of the National Catholic Rural Life Conference for twenty years. Vincent A. Yzerman, his biographer, called Liguitti "Mr. Rural Life" in the Catholic Church of the United States. Liguitti ended his career in Rome as the Vatican's permanent observer at the Food and Agricultural Organization of the United Nations, traveled extensively throughout the world lecturing, writing, and even personally showing Italian farmers how to plant a new hybrid form of corn. Liguitti humorously commented upon the Vatican rumor and gossip mills by quoting a Roman saying: "The ones who talk don't know and those who know don't talk." During the famous Vatican Council he also served as a member of the committee which wrote the revolutionary document "The Church in the Modern World". Liguitti once wrote Charlie: "I am very happy that you are accused of Communism again. After all, such accusations must come your way now and then, or you would be failing in the main purpose of your life. Keep it up, I think we'll meet a lot of Communists like you in heaven."

When Liguitti left for Rome, Charlie wrote to him in his amusing and honest style. "So here you are, once more in the air. You hardly told us that you might go, then you are gone. Tell the Holy Father in regard to the land distribution in Italy and his close advisors that there is a padre in the far West who is very anxious to see him do something about the poor peasant, or the Communists will eat them all up." Charlie hoped that Liguitti's International Rural Life Conference, "will be crowned with success and action. If something is not done to have people grow their own wheat and their own potatoes and milk their own cows and goats, I am liable to lose Faith, Hope, Charity and Patience!"

Charlie later showed a photo of a Catholic priest blessing land expropriated by the Italian government for distribution to land-less peasants to a group of seminarians and remarked, "so what does this say about your supreme rights of private property?"

Charlie's general attitude toward bishops was anything but respectful. He recognized their individual and corporate conservatism and railed against their inaction on social issues and problems with his war cry of "damned ecclesiasticism." Charlie's exception was Archbishop Mitty to whom he displayed the highest degree of respect. Archbishop Mitty was probably the best informed bishop in the West about agricultural issues and problems due to Charlie's constant stream of letters to him. Mitty, a former New York priest and U.S. Army chaplain, while he did not originate from the compost pile like Charlie, nevertheless, gave him his fullest attention and support. In a January 3rd, 1937, letter he informed the Archbishop that the conservative Commonwealth Club of San Francisco was finally taking up the issue of migratory labor. He criticized the philosophy of the Associated Farmers of California, which he described as an offshoot of the California State Chamber of Commerce. "What there are of farmers in it are large absentee landlords and the banking systems of California with the California Land Inc. leading." He went on to inform Mitty that a Father Culleton, the Vicar General of the Fresno Diocese, informed him that the Bank of America had wiped out a whole colony of Catholic Syrians through farm foreclosures. Finally, he informed Mitty that one of his rural pastors had told Charlie to stay out of his parish of Portuguese dairy farmers which Charlie intended on visiting. "They are nothing but a bunch of S.O.B.'s."

"Perhaps", retorted Charlie, "that is what the Spanish priests called the workers, the land-hungry serfs, and the peons of Mexico. Had the Church's principles of distribution of ownership of small land holdings been carried out in those Catholic countries, Communism would never have found a foothold." Finally, Charlie also suggested that Mitty send a priest to Los Banos who would assist the dairy farmers set up a cooperative. He quoted from a National Catholic Rural Life Conference Pamphlet, <u>The Popes and the Principles of Rural Life</u> in which Pope Pius X spoke to the Abbe Francois of the Diocese of Cambria in a private audience: "Tell your venerable Archbishop of the great satisfaction with which we learn that he has appointed two priests to devote themselves particularly to the farmers and their laborers. I wish that all the rural clergy knew, as well as their theology, those matters which interest the peasantry." With correspondence like this, how could Mitty not be well informed and educated about rural issues as well as be impressed by Charlie's passion for rural justice?

The priority of the National Catholic Rural Life Conference was the support and defense of the family farm where families enjoyed the pride of land ownership, healthy lives, the ability to feed themselves, and make a living. Charlie certainly transferred his own Alsatian experience and conviction that small family farms were not only possible financially, but sociologically necessary for the health of a community. He constantly battled the enemies of the small farmer, the foreclosures by banks, and corporate agricultural interests. One of his allies in this fight was the colorful Bishop of Sacramento, California, Robert Armstrong, who had previously served in the rural area of Yakima, Washington. Armstrong frequently testified for Charlie at State Legislature hearings. At one of his appearances before Senator Sheridan Downey and four other Senators, Armstrong referred to his Yakima experience where there was "an empire of homes of ten, twenty, thirty, forty, and fifty acres. There are no migratory labor problems and general conditions are a delight."

The Cooperative Movement among farmers and ranchers was a concept that Charlie preached and taught from his earliest rural experiences. He was realistic enough to know that small farmers alone could not oppose large market forces, such as packing houses, corporate farm interest, and the banks. Small farmers needed to form cooperative associations to market their products and protect themselves. "American Agriculture has suffered from the fact that it has become so highly specialized that it has more of the characteristics of an industry than of farming, particularly here in California. I believe in the individual farmer and I believe that the time is not far off when corporation or industrial farming will have to disappear just as feudal holdings disappeared in Europe and agricultural activities will be handled by farmers.

The American farmer has sunk to the level of a mere serf or peon. At best, he is today a laborer who works for somebody else. It is my belief that only to the extent that the small farmers organize and assert their rights will agriculture in the United States survive."

Charlie was a one man band not only in the San Francisco Archdiocese, but gradually in the entire state of California. Writing letters to newspapers, giving series of radio talks on station KZY, San Francisco, testifying before Federal and State legislative agricultural committees, addressing business groups, and personally organizing self–interest groups of small farmers, he played every instrument necessary to make his case. He was elected as Chairman of the California Cooperative Council where he worked with other individuals in Northern California to foster consumer and producer co-ops. Charlie was well acquainted with the famous Canadian Cooperative Education and Training Center at St. Francis Xavier University, Antigonish, Nova Scotia, as well as the Toad Lane consumer cooperative of Rochdale, England. He attempted to interest both Stanford University in Palo Alto, California, and St. Mary's College, Moraga, to set up training centers for cooperatives. In a letter to Archbishop Mitty he claimed that Stanford was bound by its charter to offer courses in consumer cooperatives. He enclosed an "evasive" letter from Stanford's President Roy Lyman Wilbur. According to Charlie, Stanford offered a course only on producer co-ops which were only feeders for packers and shippers with no control by small growers over the final sale of their products. Charlie told Mitty that the Church had a marvelous opportunity of taking the leadership in the teaching of consumer cooperatives. He had arranged a meeting through St. Mary's College President Brother Jasper with the faculty members of the Economics Department to discuss a course on cooperatives; however, nothing concrete resulted from the meeting.

Charlie was personally successful in his own organization and promotion of cooperatives beginning with the Farmers Protective League in Sebastopol, three cooperative wineries in Napa and Sonoma Counties. The two Napa groups, St. Helena and Calistoga amalgamated, while the Windsor co-op made him a lifetime honorary member. The outline and by-laws of these co-ops were drawn up in the Sebastopol parish house.

He assisted his favorite group of Portuguese dairymen in Los Banos and testified in favor of a group of small farmers of Riverside, California, to establish a cooperative electrical distribution system. Finally he was asked to help plan a conference on the Church and Cooperatives at a meeting in Oakland, California, on October 22, 1946, sponsored by the Commission of the Federal Council of Churches.

Because of his support of the Riverside electrical energy cooperative, he was invited to give the opening invocation at the Rural Electrification Administration National convention, which was held in San Francisco in February 1953. Mr. Fred Holland, Chairman of the delegates who were hosting the convention, wrote to the San Francisco Archdiocesan Chancery Office requesting that Charlie deliver the opening invocation. This procedure of asking permission for a Catholic clergyman to address a convention or large non-denominational meeting was standard operating procedure. Holland received a reply from the Chancery Office that a Father James O'Shea would give the invocation. Holland thought that there must have been some misunderstanding of his initial request for Charlie to appear, and again wrote asking for him. The acting Chancellor of the Archdiocese, Monsignor Leo T. Maher, who had assumed the administration of the Archdiocese with the illness of Archbishop Mitty, again informed Holland that O'Shea would be the innovator. This was both an insult to Charlie for his twenty year dedication to the rural life movement as well as to the delegates with whom he had worked. O'Shea, while a clerical friend and an in-house resident with Charlie at St. Mary's Parish, was an urban social worker priest in the Catholic Charities network of the Archdiocese and certainly was unfamiliar with agriculture and farmers. Why Charlie was refused remains a mystery. Had Mitty been active, there would have been no question that Charlie would have mounted the rostrum, since Mitty had openly supported Charlie's activities. Rubert Costa of Anza, California, and a Native American active in rural electrification efforts for small farmers, wrote to Charlie and expressed his dismay that the Planning Committee's request was denied. Costa explained why the delegates had first thought of Charlie. "Naturally, you were the first. Neither I or my co-delegates could think of another leading Catholic Priest who would best represent the aims of our Church as well as the work done in a practical way to make these aims a living reality in the lives of these farmers. We felt, and I believe justly so, that you employ the finest and most self-less living practical example of what our Church has done for farmers." Costa finished his letter saying that if Charlie was well and willing as he always had been to be with them, to help and bless them, why wasn't he sent to them? He was at a "complete loss" to explain Charlie's absence to his non-Catholic friends and fellow delegates. He was also irked at the way the Chancery Office handled the matter and requested that Charlie answer him. He sent his "most affectionate regards from his family, his trip, and their farm friends in Anza."

Why Maher personally refused to allow Charlie to give this invocation remains a mystery. There was no indication that Charlie and Maher had any personal clashes. It's possible that Maher didn't like Charlie's style or had heard about his "damned ecclesiastic" philosophy. In the event of Archbishop Mitty's illness Bishop Hugh Donohoe was named acting Administrator of the Archdiocese by Rome. However, Donohoe, not wanting the responsibilities of administering the day to day activities of the Church, allowed Maher to take over and operate as the manager.

Charlie, at this time, had retired and was living in residence at St. Mary's Church, Oakland. His personal letterhead described him as "Pastor Emeritus, St. Mary's Church, Oakland", and in the upper right hand corner, "Has Been for 20 years Director of the National Catholic Rural Life Conference for the Archdiocese of San Francisco." Charlie wrote to Leo Maher enclosing a copy of Costa's letter and requested that Maher clarify the Chancery Office's position on the denial. He reminded Maher that "as a matter of duty, he had made a report to Archbishop Mitty about his involvement with the rural electrification project." He also remarked how much the Farm Bureau had appreciated his efforts. He ended his letter by saying that he was "personally entitled to know why he was silenced for the invocation or was there something like a Purple Curtain?" He ended his letter with "Domine nobis pacem" ("Lord, give us peace"). A copy of this letter retrieved from the San Francisco Archdiocese Archives at St. Patrick's Seminary, Menlo Park, had this note written on the top "Answer???" There was none.

During this period Leo Maher terminated one of the most creative and novel apostolates to California farm workers, the Spanish Mission Band. Three Irish American priests Donald McDonnell, Thomas Mc-Cullough, and John Duggan along with a Portuguese American John Garcia convinced Archbishop Mitty in the Spring of 1950 of the need of a new approach the Archdiocese's agricultural counties and their farm worker communities. A "Priests' Conference on the Spanish Speaking" had been organized by Charlie Philipps, McDonnell, McCullough, and others at St. Charles Church, San Francisco, in June 1949. The purpose of the meeting was to expose the facts about the Archdiocese's Spanish Speaking communities and offer suggestions on how to best serve them.

Consequently, Archbishop Mitty in June of 1950 appointed the four to serve Spanish Speaking communities in specific counties: McDonnell to Santa Clara County, Duggan to Southern Alameda County, McCullough to San Joaquin and Stanislaus, and Garcia to Contra Costa. It was not surprising for Mitty to endorse such a new and novel apostolate. He possessed a deep sense of social justice as well as having been kept informed for years by Charlie's constant reports on agricultural and farm labor problems.

In the beginning, the Band members were to live at the major Seminary, St. Patrick's in Menlo Park, California, under the spiritual direction of Father William Sheehy, a public speaking professor. This arrangement proved ineffective because the seminary was too far from their appointed areas. Duggan moved into an old church in Decoto, California. McCullough resided at St. Mary's Church, Stockton, and served nearby labor camps. McDonnell eventually established Guadalupe Center in East San Jose in a building donated by the Mayfair Packing Company. Garcia resided in a parish in Berkeley serving the Spanish speaking neighborhoods of West Berkeley and the labor camps of Contra Costa County. Duggan was older than the other three. He had been a Christian Brother teaching Mexican boys at Cathedral High School, Los Angeles. Encouraged to study theology by the famous Philosophy

Professor James Haggerty of St. Mary's College, he entered St. Patrick's Seminary, was ordained in 1945, and was assigned to Charlie Philipps at St. Mary's Parish. Duggan grew up in the Irish Mission District of San Francisco and was influenced by the fiery sermons on labor and social justice by the famous Father Peter Yorke. The other three priests were seminary classmates. Later on Father Ronald Burke joined the Band.

The new missionaries at first were welcomed by the parish clergy in whose parishes they would be serving for lack of a trained bilingual parish clergy; however, as time passed by were criticized for their independence and also their physical appearance. The four certainly identified with the poor, were out in the dust of labor camps that reflected on their clerical clothing, and drove beat up automobiles. Many clerical critics commented on seeing them that "one doesn't have to look dirty to serve the poor", not that such men had any inclination to work with the poor.

Initially their efforts were primarily spiritual and religious, saying masses, holding religious services and education classes in Mexican labor camps and barrios. However, they soon became aware of the poverty and inhuman living conditions of farm workers and their families and began to become more socially active on their behalf.

McCullough cut an imposing figure on the streets and back roads of Stockton roaring around on a beat up Harley Davidson motor cycle. He witnessed so many problems in the labor camps: wretched living conditions, workers getting ripped off, Mexican pimps bringing their whores into the camps. He was determined to organize these workers into a labor union and contacted the AFL-CIO urging it to come to Stockton. When the union didn't respond, McCullough rented a small office in downtown Stockton and initiated the birth of a farm workers union called "AGUA". He was instructed by church authorities to cease riding his Harley around town, even though he and McDonnell took off on it to attend a national church sponsored conference for the Spanish Speaking in San Antonio, Texas. Along the way they were pulled over by a highway patrolman who was chagrined to discover that these two characters were Roman Catholic priests.

Gilbert Padilla came to Stockton to head the first CSO (Community Service Organization) community center in a hall provided by the legendary Franciscan priest Father Allan McCoy, OFM who was then Pastor of St. Mary's Church. McCoy was a quiet but solid social activist who used his parish as a training center for young Franciscan seminarians. McCullough handed over his nascent union to Padilla, whose salary had been secured through John Duggan's connections with Chicago Monsignor Bill Quinn of the National Bishops Committee for The Spanish Speaking. Finally, forces were able to convince the AFL-CIO to assume the effort and AWOC (Agricultural Workers Organizing Committe-AFL-CIO) was formed under the direction of a veteran crafts union organizer Norman Smith. Padilla in later years would emphasize that long before the rise of Cesar Chavez and the creation of the UFW(United Farm Workers) union, the Catholic Church in the form of a Catholic priest (McCullough) had initiated a farm workers' union.

Down in Santa Clara county McDonnell was working in the poor barrio in East San Jose called "Sal Si Puedes" ("Get Out if You Can") and trying to build a church community in the poverty stricken neighborhood. There he met a young farm worker Cesar Chaver whom he enlisted to assist him both in San Jose and nearby farm labor camps where he offered Mass and religious services. Richard Creswald de Castillo and Richard Garcia in their historical portrait: <u>Cesar Chavez: A Triumph of Spirit,</u> described McDonnell's influence in shaping Cesar's social conscience. He was encouraged to study the Papal Social Encyclicals, labor history, the teaching of St. Francis of Assisi, and the life of Ghandi, all of which made a deep impression on the young farm worker.

About the same time, a 45 year old community organizer, Fred Ross, was looking for a candidate to train for organizing Mexican communities. Ross was a lead organizer in the famous Saul Alinsky's Industrial Areas Foundation, Chicago, whose goal was to train community leaders of poor neighborhoods for political change. Ross came first to Los Angeles, a community with the second largest number of Mexicans in the world, and organized the successful Community Service Organization (CSO). Following victories in Los Angeles, he decided to develop CSO chapters in highly impacted California Mexican communities. Arriving in San Jose he asked Father McDonnell to identify some young Chicanos with leadership potential. The name Cesar Chavez was suggested, and Ross's meeting with Cesar sowed the seeds of not only political power for Mexican American communities of the 50's but also of the future United Farm Workers Organization (UFW).

Cesar's first solo organization campaign was in St. Mary's Parish, Oakland. At Ross's suggestion, he contacted me, and I helped him organize his house meeting, although I hadn't the slightest idea about what he was trying to do. In fact I didn't attend the meeting. Years later I read with guilt feelings Cesar's description of this meeting in Jacques Levy's Cesar Chavez. Autobiography of La Causa. "When Father Cox set up the first house meeting for me, he didn't go, he just called a lady and set it up in West Oakland." I did help him set up other meetings which led to the general meeting of 368 people in St. Mary's social hall and the founding of the first CSO chapter in Oakland. My association with Cesar led to my later involvement with the farm workers movement and a long friendship with Cesar.

On January 5th, 1961, McDonnell and McCullough traveled to the San Diego Diocese and met with Bishop Buddy to inform him that they planned to attend a joint AWOC-UPWA labor meeting in Calexico where McDonnell delivered an invocation and led the workers in singing a hymn. The upshot of their presence was that some local growers reported them to Bishop Buddy for leading the workers in Communist songs and stirring them up. They were also partially to blame for the lettuce strike that soon followed. Buddy immediately called Leo Maher who quickly summoned the four Mission Band priests and immediately transferred them to individual parishes. Maher conducted no investigation of the charges and allowed no recourse, but worse, there was no outcry from individual groups such as CSO or the AFL-CIO with whom they had cooperated.

John Duggan who had accepted an assignment with the American Bishops Committee on the Spanish Speaking, living in Chicago and working the midwest, wrote a scorching letter to Bishop Donohoe, personally attacking and criticizing him for his inactivity in thwarting Maher's actions. Donohoe had once been the professor of Social Ethics at St. Patrick's Seminary, the major seminary of the Archdiocese, and was known as the Church's spokesperson on labor and social issues. Later, Maher was elevated as the Bishop of the newly created Diocese of Santa Rosa in Northern California and subsequently as Bishop of San Diego, California, where he died.

Interestingly Charlie served as a mentor and advisor to the Spanish Mission Band. Occasionally the members would assemble with Charlie in his study at St. Mary's and share their experiences with him. One piece of advice that he gave them was to watch their backs that the hierarchy did not scuttle their activities. Apparently they didn't look close enough. McCoullugh was relegated to an urban parish in Berkeley, California, where he tried to adapt to the life style of the local clergy, including playing golf. Duggan always claimed that McCullough never got over the Band's break up. McDonnell went to learn Japanese in Japan and worked later as a missionary in Brazil flying around in his own plane, "The Spirit of St. Patrick," visiting Japanese immigrant farmers who had married Brazilian Catholic women. Garcia adjusted to a parish in Contra Costa County, and Burke went off to work with indigenous people in the Guatemalan highlands, until he quickly retuned to San Francisco after learning that his name was on a "death" list. Duggan returned to California and worked as the Pastor of St. Gertrude Church, Stockton, California, from where he left the priesthood, married Sally Villanueva, a nurse and one of his parishioners. Both left Stockton to join Cesar Chavez in Delano and work for the United Farm Workers. Before his death several years ago, McCullough told me that even with the demise of the Band, it was time for it to dissolve. I disagreed with him that while religious figures, bishops, priests, nuns, and committed lay people vividly supported Chavez and the development of the UFW, no priest presence afterwards entered the many farm labor camps of California. The establishment had snuffed out the most meaningful religious witness to California farm workers. John and Sally Duggan eventually retired to live in Meadow Vista, California, and remained active in community and civil rights causes. Duggan passed away at age 89 on June 8th, 2005.

One of the many hilarious stories about McDonnell's return to the States was related to me by Tom McCullough at my home in Richmond,

California. I had intended on writing a history of the Band and invited him to our home for dinner and an interview. McDonnell was ready to return to the States and the Archdiocese of San Francisco. He asked McCullough to come down to Brazil and help him fly "The Spirit of St. Patrick" back to the States. Both priests were taught to fly by a crop duster pilot in Stockton who had some unusual moves not taught in most flying schools, such as dropping a wing, falling directly down, and then suddenly pulling out of the dive, and coming to a landing. The two priests left Brazil, headed North over South America, and then flying low over the Florida straits, realized that they were running low on fuel. Luckily their Irish Guardian Angel helped them to notice an air strip on which they landed.

Slowly coming to a stop they peered out the windows to see themselves surrounded by military vehicles and jeeps with military personnel pointing automatic weapons at them. Unbeknownst to them, they had invaded a Strategic Air Command base (SAC) by flying undetected under the radar system of the base. The jeeps led them to the office of the commanding officer who just happened to be a Roman Catholic. McDonnell and McCullough introduced themselves as two Catholic priests. The Commander, chagrined that his base had been invaded, instructed his troops to gas up the two padres and then told them in no uncertain terms "to get the hell off his base and not tell anyone about the episode."

The ravages of World War II left the farms of Europe in shambles; homes, barns, equipment, land, and particularly livestock had been destroyed by attacking and retreating armies. Building materials and farm equipment were more easily available than livestock for the rebirth of European agricultural communities. Meanwhile, Charlie had received some interesting correspondence from Alsace on December 26th, 1944, from a U.S. Army Corporal named Herbert Heintze. World War II hostilities had separated Charlie from contact with his Alsace family. Heintze stated that his letter "will no doubt come to you like a bolt from the blue." He informed Charlie that he was presently quartered in Charlie's home with his nephew Charles Philipps after American troops took over his village. He wrote to inform him of his family's welfare.

His priest brother was actively engaged in his parish nearby. His sister Marie Adele had died in 1943, and another sister-nun Aloise was enjoying good health. His other nephew, formerly a machine gunner in the French Army, had been forced into the German army in 1940 and was on the Russian front. Many of the men of the village were forced to leave with the enemy to go into the "Volkstrum". The village was practically undamaged as a result of the hasty retreat of the occupying German forces. The Philipps family sent their greetings to Charlie in hopes that he could visit them when the war was over.

Heintze also wrote Charlie from Werl Wasfalen, Germany, in June 1945 telling him that he had received a letter from Charlie's nephew, Charles Philipps. He regretted that the U.S. 79th Division troops had to fall back and leave the peaceful little village. "It was such a quiet little Dorf, nestled in among the hills and in its wintery setting made a peaceful place to spend Christmas. They also held and battled some of Hitler's best to a standstill further back in Alsace for which the Division received a Presidential citation." The Philipps' family were alive and well, but the town was badly damaged and the family home partly destroyed. Heintze proceeded to describe the utter destruction of German cities. "Everything is completely smashed with the people individually and collectively so destroyed that they don't know where to turn, and see no help forthcoming on earth, they are turning to their God without interference from the Gestapo."

Heintze ended his letter on a humorous note, telling Charlie that his nephew came to him complaining that soldiers from a nearby ack-ack unit were killing his chickens. He ended by calling himself "Heartless Heintze" because of the many evil things he had done in the service of his country such as finding billets for 140 men.

Charlie attempted to locate Heintze. A February 7th, 1947, communiqué from the War Department, Office of the Adjutant General, Washington D.C. to Charlie stated "Herbert F. Heintze, 37379573, was separated from the Army of the United States at which time he gave his address for future reference as c/o Bon 65 Park Terrace East, New York, N.Y." It is not known whether Charlie was successful in contacting him or not.

The end of World War II hostilities provided Charlie with an opportunity of reuniting himself with his Alsatian roots and involving himself enthusiastically with the Heifer Project International, sponsored by the Church of the Brethren whose purpose was to restock the destroyed cattle herds of Europe. Charlie, in an August 18, 1945, letter to Monsignor Liguitti, National Director of the Catholic Rural Life Conference, described the first direct message he had received from his sister in Alsace at the end of the war. His whole family survived the three battles around his village of Stundwiller in Northern Alsace. Three-fourths of the homes and barns were destroyed. His nephew who lived in the original family home had lost a barn, his cattle, and several rooms in the old house. Charlie described his plan of shipping heifers to every one of the fifty families in his village. He even thought of flying to Alsace to begin the coordination of the project; however, lack of shipping facilities prevented him from completing his plans. Liguitti advised Charlie to work with the Brethren's program.

The Heifer Project was born in the mind of Dan West, a young Brethren lay reader and relief worker with the American Friends Service Committee during the Spanish Civil War (1937-38). Recognizing the short supply of powdered milk for children in Spain, West proposed shipping dairy cattle to restock the Spanish farms. Upon his return to Illinois in 1938, he submitted his proposal and a Volunteer Committee was formed to promote "Heifers for Relief". The idea gained enthusiasm and support throughout the Brethren Communities. With the end of World War II hostilities, the United Nations formed a special agency, United Nations Relief and Rehabilitation Administration (UNRRA). UNRRA agreed to provide cattle transportation to Europe on the condition that the Brethren take responsibility for recruiting livestock attendants for all shipments. Consequently, thousands of Brethren Volunteers and elders served as "seagoing cowboys" on the ships. While the Heifer Project operated under the direction of the B.S.C., other religious organizations were invited to join the Heifer Committee: The American Baptist Church, United Church of Christ, Methodist Commission on Overseas Relief, the Mennonite Central Committee, and the National Catholic Rural Life Conference. A Heifer Project central office was opened in the newly acquired Brethren Service Center in New Windsor, Maryland. The response of the religious community was overwhelming. Cattle came in by the thousands, and the farm of Roger Roop, near Union Bridge, Maryland, was rented as a holding center. Cattle were shipped to piers in Baltimore, Newport News, and Atlanta. Additional centers were established in Ohio, Indiana, and Wisconsin.

Clara T. Johnson, author of <u>Milk for the World</u>: <u>The Heifer Project on the West Coast</u>: <u>A Story of Love in Action,</u> chronicled the development of the Brethren's West Coast Heifer Project activities from its center in Modesto, California. Johnson stated, "The West Coast Committee decided that cows were neither Catholic or Protestant and that a Catholic member would be a valuable asset. Father Philipps of Oakland was asked to join the committee. Philipps was a real promoter, and he thought Heifers for Relief was one of the sanest, down to earth, programs in existence. He explained it as the cycle of life: Milk, meat, and manure. He was instrumental in securing the cooperation of the Portuguese dairy men on the West side of the county, and at one of their big celebrations, they constructed a corral at the Church, bringing in their donated animals and holding an auction with the proceeds going to Heifers for Relief. Father Philipps was not able to be present at many committee meetings, but his enthusiasm and promotional emphasis is remembered by all who worked with him."

The editorial of the <u>Sacramento Herald</u>, the California Catholic Diocesan newspaper, by editor Patrick Quinlan stated, "that while fifty percent of the cattle given to date represent donations of midwest people, this unique approach to relief is also known on the Pacific Coast. The Reverend Charles Philipps, Rural Life Director of the Archdiocese of San Francisco and Pastor of St. Mary's Church, Oakland, is collecting and shipping substantial numbers of cattle. Heifers from California will soon graze on foreign fields and support needy families."

Charlie was "calling in" his chips from all the rural parishes and communities such as Houghson, Rodeo, and Stockton. His work with the Los Banos Dairymen's Cooperative Union resulted in fourteen heifers being pledged along with free alfalfa plus free veterinarian's vaccinations. To finance his efforts, Charlie wrote to Philip Murray, National

President of the AFL-CIO, for financial assistance from local councils. "Ever since last January when the battle was raging to three months around my village and neighborhood," he wrote, "I know that the cattle would be eaten, stolen, or destroyed." His fears were confirmed by recent correspondence, and he stated that "he was trying to get together somewhere between fifty and one hundred heifers."

Perhaps no project of Charlie's many activities had been more memorialized and quoted than his appearance at St. Patrick's Seminary, Menlo Park, California, to address the seminarian student body about "Heifers for Europe" and afterwards to dine at the faculty table of the student dining room. Charlie had previously inspired and regaled the students by saying that "all of my heifers are going over pregnant". Since only a few of the faculty professors had attended his lecture, Charlie was seated next to the Seminary Rector, Father Thomas Mulligan. Charlie began the dinner by describing his heifer project. Mulligan, originally an Iowa farm boy in his youth, had been chosen to tighten up a seminary that had become somewhat loose. Narrow-minded, devoid of any sense of humor, and prone to explosive outbursts of temper, an obsessive-compulsive with a spirituality that reflected that of the "Flagelatti", he was grist in Charlie's mill when he turned to Philipps and said, "Father Philipps, this project seems very admirable, but wouldn't it be much more practical to ship tractors and farm equipment to Europe?" Charlie stunned by Mulligan for a moment answered, "Well, Father Mulligan, that is not a bad idea, but the fact is that tractors don't shit!" Mulligan's blood rushed to his bald pate. He turned away in anger from Charlie and refused to speak to him for the rest of the meal. Naturally this quote soon filtered down to the student body and entered the currents of clerical tradition. Like "Remember the Alamo!" or "Hannibal is at the gates?" whenever in future years Charlie's name and memory were mentioned, "Tractors don't shit!" had to rank as one of his most famous proclamations.

The San Francisco News headline of December 25, 1936, announced: "Farmers ask Laws to Curb Union Labor." The article described the efforts of the Associated Farmers of California to introduce legislation in the California State Legislature which would oppose unionization of agricultural workers or the closed shop preferential hiring for agriculture. The bill would also forbid residence in the State by illegal aliens as well as relief to strikers and other people who "refused to accept work at the prevailing wage." In a report to the National Catholic Welfare Conference (the national headquarters of the American Bishops in Washington, D.C.), Charlie reported on the efforts by employer groups to break up the strongly organized packing shed workers. "It is my belief that the employers were bound to break up the future organization of field workers and pickers, the majority of whom are Filipinos, Mexicans, and Japanese, and prevent the organization of agricultural laborers." Charlie's support of union organizing efforts in his Sebastopol parish put him in a box of supporting the small farmers as well as the workers who picked their crops. He was frequently stopped in downtown Sebastopol and asked, "Well, Father Philipps, how are your peasants today?"

Grower groups across the country also attempted to gain control and operate the Federal constructed labor camps of contract workers from Mexico. The State of California had 20 such camps valued at six million dollars. In an April 23, 1948, letter to Reverend John Birch, Director of the U.S. Bishops Committee for the Spanish Speaking, Charlie sent articles from <u>The San Francisco Chronicle</u> newspaper columnist Stanton Delapane, which described the general conditions of migratory labor in Northern California. Charlie described Delapane's series as reading like "a new edition of the <u>Grapes of Wrath</u>". He went on to also describe the political issue of who was to buy, own, and run the 21 Federal Camps in California. "As Rural Life Director," he said, "I advocated their purchase and operation by the State. I was supported by the Grange, the AFL-CIO, and other social minded groups." California State Senator Harry E. Drobish of Bangor, California, wrote to Charlie on April 24, 1950, informing him that SB 2246 which provided for the continued ownership of Federally built migrant camps, had been passed in the last few days of both Houses of Congress and signed by the President. Drobish described the legislation as "one of the initial milestones passed on the road to social progress in behalf of minority groups in agriculture." The Senator ended his letter by telling Charlie that he would "be invited by the Public Housing Administration in Washington, D.C.

to a meeting in Sacramento to discuss plans on how to carry out the housing program at the grass roots."

Charlie attended a seminar on the Spanish Speaking of the West and Southwest in San Antonio Texas, July 20-23, 1943. He wrote to Archbishop Mitty giving him the synopsis of Archbishop Lucey's speech on the exploitation of the Mexican population. Charlie voiced his reaction to the speech in his letter to Archbishop Mitty: "The Church should take its prayer, the Confiteor, of self confession seriously and instead of fighting Communism or Liberalism, the admission of its inaction could result in a conversion towards social action. I still have my misgivings about what the Church has done or rather neglected to do for these underprivileged people." In the same letter he asked Mitty why Catholic Religious orders, originally instituted primarily to serve the poor, always wound up running high class colleges and universities which are little different than secular finishing schools, with emphasis on one's personal salvation, a very selfish feature, with little regard for social responsibility. He also informed Archbishop Mitty that he was cooperating with the local Pan American Association which took an interest in Mexican nationals working on the railroads and living in labor camps. He also allowed the organization the use of his social hall for its social gatherings.

Charlie's interest and support of California agricultural workers was evidenced in his criticism of the importation of field workers from Mexico, the "bracero" program and the effort by the Agricultural Section of the California State Chamber of Commerce to deny suitable wages to California workers, claiming that Texas and Florida wages prevented California producers from paying better wages. He attended the Agricultural and Cannery Worker Conference in San Francisco, February 27-28, where the issues of the meeting related to farm labor conditions in California. In his report of the conference to Archbishop Mitty Charlie stated that the "agricultural worker makes a very fine interstate football". He also observed that "the days of the craft unions were numbered because the leadership was from the top down and ignored the lower strata of labor. With shades of the future Mission Band of four priests assigned to work with farm labor in the San Francisco Archdiocese, Charlie urged Mitty to assign some young priests to work with the labor movement in San Francisco and Oakland. Finally, he mentioned that he met and shook hands for the first time with an out and out Socialist, a Mr. Doss, the Secretary of the Fruit and Vegetable Union of Salinas, as well as an out and out Communist, a young woman graduate of one of our convents.

Charlie's other post war activities included his participation in CROP, Christian Relief Overseas Program. Sponsored nationally by the Catholic Rural Life Conference, Church World Service, and Lutheran World Relief, their motto was "You can plant a crop every year, but people die of starvation only once." The purpose of the program was to collect grains, soy beans, and dairy products from rural church people and send these overseas to alleviate post war starvation. Charlie organized meetings in all of the rural counties of the Archdiocese. He was assisted in his organizing efforts by Mr. James O'Connell, a Sebastopol, California, a long time friend.

BIG GROWERS/SMALL FARMERS

❦

*M*ark Reisner's epic treatment of water issues in the West, Cadillac Desert, describes the development of California's Central Valley Project. Once a dry and barren wasteland, and now a rich garden of agriculture made possible through the miracle of irrigated water, the Central Valley is a 400 mile long, 60 mile wide, north to south stretch of Central California, home to 5.5 million people, and the greatest garden in the world which supplies one quarter of America's food production. Historically agriculture has been the major contributor in this area not only of food production but also of political power and profit that has generated a history of cheap State and Federal handouts to the agricultural industry.

These lush fields were not always evident. Originally valley farmers prior to World War I irrigated fields of wheat and cattle through a series of canals and sluice ways cut from rivers and streams. With the invention of the centrifugal pump, they had access to the valley's apparent (to them) unlimited water from the shallow aquifers which may have held three quarters of a billion acre feet of water. By 1930 a million and half acres of land were being irrigated in the San Joaquin Valley with a system of 23,000 well pipes sunk in the ground. Farmers were drawing up so much water that the water table dropped 300 feet in some areas. The aquifer was predicted to dry up in 30 to 40 years. Groundwater in California of which 80 percent is used by agriculture is unregulated as it is in most states. So, in 1933 the agricultural community pulled together its political and financial power to create the Central Valley Project, one of the largest financial gifts to California's farmers from State and Federal governments which has continued to flow to the present day. At its inauguration the CVP was the largest water distribution system in the world, taking water from the State's northern reservoirs, the Shasta Dam on the upper Sacramento River and Trinity Lake on the Trinity River, and sending it south through the Sacramento River to the Sacramento Delta where massive sized pumps move it along through a series of pumping stations through hundreds of miles of canals south.

The Central Valley Project was one of the major agricultural battles which Charlie fought. Supporters and opponents lined up early between large growers and their allies, California Chamber of Commerce, Associated Farmers of America, and the giant private utility company the Pacific Gas and Electric Company. Against them stood small farmers, the California Grange, religious groups, and public/nonprofit utility companies independent of the large PG&E.

The urgent need for additional water on the part of Southern San Joaquin Valley farm interests initiated an investigation for future water supplies by the California State Legislature in 1931. The Central Valley Project Act was passed by the Legislature in 1933 as a major part of the State Water Plan. The Act created a Water Project Authority to construct and operate a system of works for the development, distribution, and sale of water and electric power in the Sacramento and Joaquin Valleys. The Act also included the construction of Shasta and Friant Dams, the San Joaquin pumping system, and the Contra Costa, Madera, and Friant-Kern canals. The generation, sale, and distribution of electric energy were also included.

Due to the economic conditions of the mid-thirties, the State of California had to seek construction funds from the Federal Government. Federal monies were secured under the National Industrial Act of 1933 and involved the Federal Bureau of Reclamation, which opened an office in Sacramento, the State Capitol, to supervise the operation. The costs of the CVP were to be reimbursed by the sale of irrigated water and electrical power. While history and the law definitely established the project primarily as an irrigation effort, some federal administrators viewed it as a federally owned and administered commercial power system with irrigation as a secondary purpose. The first Federal Regional Director at Sacramento, Charles E. Carrey, an electrical engineer, stated on one occasion that the CVP was a power development, not an irrigation plan.

The social policies inherent in the federal operation was the promotion of the family size farms and the limitation of the delivery of water to not more than 160-acres in a single ownership or 320 acres in the case of husband and wife ownership. Secondly, the Act provided for the public ownership of power distribution systems in order to make low price power available. Acreage determination and power preferences determined who should be the beneficiaries of the project, who should own the distribution facilities, and who should distribute the benefits.

Acreage limitation in Federal projects was not a new concept. Before Congress could adopt the Reclamation Act of 1902, it had to make social policy decisions regarding the beneficiaries of publicly subsidized projects and the type of rural society it wished to encourage. Congress was guided by policies developed much earlier in the distribution of public lands such as the Pre-emption Act of 1841 and the Homestead Act of 1862. "No right to use the water for land in private ownership shall be sold for a tract exceeding 160-acres to one landowner." The Clause, affirmed in principle thirteen times since 1902, firmly opposed land monopoly in favor of the farmer who personally worked the land.

The Reclamation Act had three interrelated objectives:

1. To provide homes and economic opportunities for as many families as possible;
2. To ensure a wide distribution of benefits by curtailing land speculations made more valuable through irrigation;
3. To encourage the development of family farm communities.

The Federal Government in the Reclamation Act of 1902 assumed responsibility for the development of the nation's water supplies and viewed its role as an extension of the earlier homestead laws, which gave a limit of 160-acres to any one individual. Senator Hansbrough (ND) introducing the Homestead Act on February 2, 1902, remarked, "Mr. President, the purpose of this measure is to assist in providing homes for the increasing population of the country." Senator Francis G. Newland of Nevada stated that the purpose of the Bill was to guard against land monopoly and hold land in small tracts for the support of a family. President Franklin D. Roosevelt, in support of the Central Valley Project funding, remarked that "our people as a whole will profit, for successful home building is but another name of the upbuilding of the nation." Finally, the Democratic Administration's New Deal targeted the family farm as a policy goal and developed an entire agency, The Farm Security Administration, to work on behalf of the family farm.

The State of California had argued over land policies for years. The scarcity of public lands for settlement due to early Mexican land grants and later Federal grants of land to railroads, set the controversy over land policy that has lasted for 100 years. California in 1850 argued over being a slave versus a free state, later the importation of Chinese labor, and land monopoly curbs in the State Constitution. The 160-acre limitation was one more historical argument over what kind of rural society California should adopt.

Large landowners and corporate agricultural interests claimed that California could best develop its agriculture through large owners and cheap farm labor. The Bureau of Agricultural Economics conducted a 1945 study, which showed that fifty-three percent of the irrigable land in Madera, Tulare, and Kern Counties was in farms over 320 acres and that fewer than five percent of the total landowners owned these holdings. A California Labor Federation statement in 1959 cited that three percent of the landowners in the San Joaquin Valley owned fifty-two percent of the land. Many holdings exceeded 10,000 acres and several other 100,000 acres. The Kern County Land Company alone owned 178,997 acres. 1947 testimony on SB 912 hearings, a bill to exempt the Central Valley from the acreage limitation of the law, showed that the land issue was a major one.

Opponents of corporate agriculture such as the California Grange, Veterans Groups, religious and labor organizations argued that small farmers could best develop California's agriculture and that the division of wealthy owners and poor agricultural laborers was not beneficial. Harry Joseph Hogan in his doctoral thesis The 160-acre Limitation:

Conflict for Value Systems in the Federal Reclamation Program refers to the myth of the family farm, which had been perpetuated in American culture and government policy toward rural America. Inherent in the myth is the belief that the countryside has an economic, social, and moral superiority over the city. Hogan claims that the family farm ideal was an importation of the idyllic European peasant farm, which was nothing more than a subsistence farm unable to compete as an economic unit in agriculture.

The superiority of the country over the city was a prevalent view of the East Coast in the middle 1800's. The country was pictured as a garden of innocence and virtue, while the city remained a den of sin and corruption. Guidebooks for immigrant Irish newcomers urged them to settle on the rural frontier where work was better, a man could preside over his own homestead and watch a growing and prosperous family. Catholic fiction of the times supported this romantic ideal. Author Mary Sadlier in her 1860 novel Con O'Regan or Emigrant Life in the New World wrote that "the city was the scene of evil while everything good took place on the farm. Patsy Bergen used to skip her catechism class in the city, but led a life of virtue on the farm." The legendary Archbishop of New York City, John Hughes, in an emotional speech to an Irish audience in Cork, described the state of Irish immigrants in America, as owners of 300 acres of land in the West instead of a humble cottage in Ireland.

Charlie's identification with the small farmer had his roots in his peasant background about which he boasted. While he may have idealized the social values of the family farm, he also had a realistic view of the farm as a successful economic enterprise. Charlie distinguished growers from farmers. Corporate farming was identified by huge land holdings, packing houses, shipping, and retail outlets. The independent or family farmer lived on or near his land and operated it himself. Charlie often said that it was a mistake to imply that "Bigness" was the secret to efficient and productive farming. The independent farms were productive and profitable enough to support a family adequately.

However, he warned that because packers and carriers determined prices for products, the family farmer was in danger. The price for products had not increased in years, a fact supported by the California State Grange. The Fifty-Seventh Annual Session of the Grange at Redding, California, October 15-18, 1929, reported that California farmers were enjoying greater prosperity and receiving better prices that in 1928. One year later, October 21-24,1930, at the Fifty Eighth Session in Napa, the Grange continued to fight for farmers' price support stating, "We have witnessed in some parts of the State today a depression in prices of crops unparalleled in the history of the State." The delegates went on to resolve that their members should militate to bring about an equalization between prices paid to the producer and those charged to the consumer.

Prior to the authorization of Congress to underwrite the Central Valley Project, arguments and political maneuvering seesawed over which Federal agency, the Bureau of Reclamation or the Army Corps of Engineers, should construct and monitor the projects. Water and utility interests, corporate farmers, and the Chamber of Commerce were allied against supporters of the small farmer and the non-profit-municipal utility companies. Both Federal departments had different social objectives. Reclamation proposed the widest degree of Federal land distribution among small land owners as well as the most attractive power rates for rural and urban consumers. The Corps, whose priority was flood control and navigation, had zero social objectives. As a unit of the Department of the Interior, Reclamation was directly responsible to the President and Congress, while the Corps was monitored by a Congressional Committee. Corporate agriculture and groups supporting State control of the CVP opted for the Corps, since the average limitation and anti-land speculation provisions of the Reclamation Law would not apply under Corps' supervision. Likewise, the preferences for small farmers and nonprofit utility groups would not be considered. Actually the Corps preferred private utility companies to develop power projects rather than small agricultural groups or nonprofit rural electrification units. Because of the power features of the CVP Act, the giant utility monopoly Pacific Gas and Electric Company (PG&E) financed a ballot referendum in the State elections of 1933 in an attempt to defeat the establishment of the CVP. The effort was defeated. Presidents Roosevelt and Truman both supported and enforced the provisions of the Reclamation Law.

The California State Grange in their annual state meetings from 1934 to 1936 had criticized the high utility rates paid to private utility companies by farmers. Farmers in Tulare and other counties, for example, were paying 50% of their gross income for power. The Grange filed petitions with the Railroad Commission asking for reduced power rates against the Southern California Edison Company, Pacific Gas and Electric Company, San Joaquin Light and Power, and the Great Western Power Company. The 1934 Session of the Grange reported that "since 1931 it had opposed the development of water and power resources by private interests and advocated the support of publicly owned districts by farmer groups."

Charlie leapt into the land and energy fight with relish and enthusiasm against the powers of agribusiness and private companies. One of his first battles was his three page rebuttal of the famous owner and editor of The San Francisco Chronicle, George Cameron, who wrote a lengthy February 14, 1947, editorial "Acreage Limitation Unjustified". Charlie stated that Cameron's editorial was prejudicial against a long standing effort of the National Catholic Rural Life Conference's support of the Federal Government's wide distribution of land ownership and described Cameron's "Considerable amount of misstatements of facts." He ended his letter by suggesting that the Editor correct his information and attitude towards the 160-acre limitation.

Charlie admitted that he was fighting for the small family farmer as more and more California land was falling into corporate hands. Stockton's State Senator Bradford Crittenden was quoted in a June 1944 San Francisco Examiner saying that "the Federal Government was laying plans to set up a socialistic communistic agricultural program in California." Charlie sent out letters supporting the 160-acre limitation. He arranged for Bishop Robert Armstrong of Sacramento to appear in support of the limitation before hearings in the State Legislature. Armstrong cited his former experience in the Washington State Yakima Valley where the 160-acre limitation was successful. "These farmers have an empire of homes with farms of thirty, forty, and fifty acres.

There are no migratory problems and general conditions are a delight." Armstrong and Charlie became close friends through their personal commitment to family farmers. Armstrong thanked Charlie for his efforts by writing, "The Reclamation Bureau has a fight on its hands with the big landowners and your support will be appreciated." Charlie's humorous note to Archbishop Mitty described his Sacramento dinner at Armstrong's house following Charlie's participation in a Protestant Church Rural Life meeting in Davis, California. "Bishop Armstrong invited me to his residence to talk over some aspects of the Central Valley Project and the 160-acre limitation. Whatever taint of Protestantism I may have acquired, he had me wash it away with a Manhattan and a bottle of wine."

Charlie congratulated a Mr. Skillen for his article "Water, Water". His October 12th, 1948, letter pointed out that Federal financing of the CVP made the project possible because of the State's inability to fund it. "Now," he lamented, "the Holy Father comes along, according to the daily news, stating that government financing is bad for people." Finally, he comments that he has been called a Socialist and a Communist. "So was Rural Life for advocating family farms."

Congressman John H. Tolan from Alameda County answered Charlie's letter regarding the five million dollar appropriation for the King's River Dam. Tolan, Chairman of the Committee of National Defense Migration, had to keep his eye on wide distributed land in the CVP. "Why returning veterans or anyone else cannot live on 160-acres of irrigated land is beyond me. So far, Father, you speak my language."

On April 24th, 1948, Charlie, as Director of the California Catholic Rural Life Conference, appeared before a Water and Power Convention in Governor's Hall, Sacramento. The meeting was held under the auspices of the Central Valley Project Conference. Charlie's remarks summed up his philosophy of rural life and his defense of the small grower. He unanimously supported the comprehensive plan of the Bureau of Reclamation to harness all of the underdeveloped water of the Central Valley. Rebuking State bureaucrats who traveled to Washington, D.C. at State expense to lobby against the CVP plan, Charlie advocated a private public power grid for California and the West and warned about private utility companies' plots to thwart public power development. He also took a strong stand against the Army Corps of Engineers invading the conservation field, particularly in the assignment of the Corps to the Pine Flat, Isabella, and Folsom Dams projects. To allow the military into economic and political life was a dangerous step. The Corps was not bound by Reclamation Bureau's protective clauses and was supported by large private land and utility interests. Charlie also urged the support of the family farm and printed out the efforts of corporate and absentee landowners to destroy and nullify the forty-six year old 160-acre provision of the Reclamation Law. Finally, his presentation urged groups and individuals to support a State water and energy policy that would assure low cost rates for farms, cities, and industries. "Large self-seeking power and land interests are betraying our State in its present crisis and planning to sell out its golden opportunity for future greatness." Charlie fought the issue down to the end. He persuaded Monsignor Liguitti, National Director of the Catholic Rural Life Conference, to urge Monsignor William O'Grady, Executive Chairman of the National Catholic Welfare Conference, Washington, D.C., representing the Catholic Bishops of the United States to appear before Congress with Charlie's notes.

The early years of the CVP, while delivering a permanent source (excluding droughts) of water to the Central Valley System, at the same time seriously ruined the State's ecosystem. Environmental awareness and activity had not yet awakened so that all kinds of damage resulted such as drained and diked wetlands detrimental to migratory wild life, pollutant runoffs from farms and cities entering the waterways, and the blockage of salmon and other fish completing their historic voyage from the sea to enter their spawning grounds. City dwellers did not comprehend the relationship between the fishing fleets of San Francisco, Fort Bragg, and Crescent City as the salmon industry went belly up and was forced to self impose a rationing period on salmon fishing. The Fall of 1992 saw 300 of the 350 salmon boats in Fort Bragg with "for sale" signs on them.

The pressure of the environmentalists led Congress to pass the Reclamation Reform Act of 1982 which took 800,000 acre feet of water from agriculture and dedicated it to wetlands and fisheries, the first re-allocation since the CVP Act was passed. The Act also raised the acre-age limitation to 960 acres as well as ended the residency requirements which were never really enforced in the Central Valley. The original Act intended the establishment of small farms occupied by family resident farmers. The Bureau of Reclamation, once the mentor of the family farm, gradually capitulated to powerful agricultural political forces. It continued to overlook abuses and allowed lands exceeding 960 acres to receive subsidized water as long as they were held in trusts or other partnerships. Charlie's fight and defense of the small family farmer had long gone down in defeat.

Glenn Martin in The San Francisco Chronicle article of October 23, 2005, "Big Shift In Flow of Water Policy", described that after 50 years of legal infighting "a victor has emerged in California's water wars...... Agriculture." The article indicated that Central Valley farmers were presently signing contracts that assured their farms of ample subsi-dized water for the next 25 to 50 years at prices far below those paid by urban areas. 200 contracts have been approved and 50 more are pend-ing. Farmers who receive Federal water are generally charged a fraction of the free-market rate. The Westland District, for example, will pay $31 per acre foot while Marin County residents in Northern California will pay $500 for Russian River water and Southern California cities will pay $200. An acre foot is approximately the amount of water used by 2 families of 5 in one year. It is interesting to note that critics of the Reclamation Act in the 1930's thought that the 40 year contract period was too long and the water rates, devoid of any rate adjustments to meet increasing project costs, were too low.

The Natural Resources Defense Council, self described as the "na-tion's most effective environmental action organization using law, sci-ence, and the support of its one million members and on-line activists to protect the planet's wildlife and wild places and insure a safe and healthy environment for all living things", is expected to file suit against these agricultural water districts, if these water contracts are approved. Charlie would have been part of the organization and the suit.

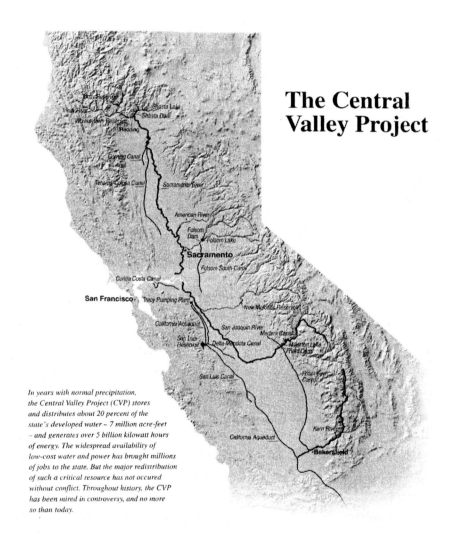

The Central Valley Project

In years with normal precipitation,
the Central Valley Project (CVP) stores
and distributes about 20 percent of the
state's developed water – 7 million acre-feet
– and generates over 5 billion kilowatt hours
of energy. The widespread availability of
low-cost water and power has brought millions
of jobs to the state. But the major redistribution
of such a critical resource has not occured
without conflict. Throughout history, the CVP
has been mired in controversy, and no more
so than today.

RETIREMENT AND DEATH

❧◦○◦❧

*W*hen Charlie formally retired as Pastor of St. Mary's in June, 1950, he divorced himself completely from all parish responsibility. Archbishop Mitty installed a whole new team of Pastor, John Walsh and two new assistants, Ray Thomas and myself. Charlie handed over the keys to the property, moved himself from the head of the dining room table to the lower end, and never once gave us any suggestions about how to do things around the place. There he sat surrounded by all of his "santos": his wheat germ, brown sugar ("there's no food value in white sugar"), jar of honey, and cracked wheat bread. To this day I have never eaten a piece of white bread because Charlie criticized the bread companies for extracting the natural vitamins out of the wheat and pumping in chemical ones. His suite of rooms at the top of the first floor of the priest house became his command post where he continued his lengthy correspondence and launched his attacks against the Associated Farmers of America, Pacific Gas and Electric Company (PG&E) and their efforts to snuff out rural electrification projects, against capitalism, international corporations, the federal Government's 160-acre limitation of farmland in California, the evils of corporate agriculture in their efforts to circumvent the law, and the "damned ecclesiaticism" of the Catholic Church.

His rooms consisted of a study with a large roll top desk, old easy chairs, and an accumulation of books, papers, magazines, and toy tractors strewn all over the room. Adjoining the study was a small bedroom. The toilet in the bathroom had been elevated off the floor for some reason. Charlie used to joke that while he had never been elevated to the a level of a bishop, he had his own throne. I used to creep quietly up the creaky staircase to try to avoid him. Because of his hearing problem he might not have heard anyone going by his study, but he must have felt the vibrations coming off the floor. Often he would cry out, "Is that you, Gerald"? At that point you knew you were doomed to at least a twenty minute discourse abut an article he had read or a book he had come across. John Duggan, one of his former assistants, used to sneak out down the back stairs to avoid him.

We came to enjoy Charlie's company, particularly at dinner time when he was present. He was a walking encyclopedia of Church history and could spin many a tale of former archbishops and other clergymen. He spent his time fund raising for his beloved Camp Sunshine, carrying on an active correspondence aided by his secretary Elizabeth Spread, visiting and entertaining friends. At this time he was in fairly good health so that he could get around his own. One day he came upstairs to my room and invited me downstairs to see one of his "new purchases". We went outside of the house and there parked in the driveway was the biggest and longest green Packard I had ever seen. I turned to Charlie and asked, "Is this yours?" And he answered that "he thought he had to get something heavy because of his bad heart." I wasn't aware that his heart was bothering him at the time, even though he had some heart problems years before.

During this period Charlie had developed an anemic condition which required him to make almost daily visits to the doctor for injections. He enlisted me to drive him to the doctor's office and then to wait in the parking lot. On one visit the nurse said to him "Father Philipps, you wouldn't have to come here to the office if you could arrange for someone to administer the shots at home. I could instruct someone on how to administer them." Charlie's immediate response was "Go down to the parking lot and tell that young priest in my green Packard to come up here." And so that's how I became Charlie's nurse for the next four years until I left St. Mary's in June 1955. The nurse carefully explained how I was to extract the medication in a syringe from two different bottles and also "to be careful not to get any air bubbles in which could get into Charlie's blood stream." I was frightened to death to have Charlie's health hanging on my ability to mix these two medications and administer the shot. So every day I would boil needles and syringes in the kitchen and then go up to his bedroom to give him the shot. He didn't have much flesh on him to start with and became thinner with the passing months. Often it was difficult to find a fleshy spot on his body to inject him. He never once complained and was always pleasant and receptive even if I had to awaken him.

Early in his illness he was able to spend the whole summer at the camp. During this period prior to the camp opening he recruited me to accompany him to a wholesale restaurant supply house owned by a long time Jewish friend. Charlie used to go on begging missions to obtain pots, pans, and other kitchen utensils for the camp. As we entered the store and were greeted by the owner, Charlie said in his clear voice, "I'd like you to meet Father Gerald Cox of St. Mary's. He's the only one who can stick a needle in a retired pastor's ass and get away with it!"

His 1955 "Dear Friends" letter informed his readers that in the Christmas of 1954, he was a dying man and asked them "to offer a prayer of thanks to the good Lord who has seen fit to leave me in your midst a whole year longer". He also made several trips to Notre Dame Hospital, San Francisco, for blood transfusions. He was also able to avoid returning to the hospital except for once a month transfusions of which he had 42 by this time. Twenty-two of his seminarian camp counselors had each donated a pint of blood. He tried his best to turn the management of the camp over to someone else, but it remained in his hands, and he was able to stay the entire eight weeks, "having the devotion of our voluntary cooks in the kitchen and the generous sweat of counselors of St. Patrick's Seminary ."

During this camp period the seminarians used to take turns sitting up with Charlie at night. Bill O'Donnell remembers seeing a book which Charlie had been reading and which had fallen to the floor. The book was The Confessions of St. Augustine. O'Donnell remarked to the other counselors that "this is where he must be getting his strength from".

Two years later, in an August 10, 1957, letter to the Archbishop, he reported that he was able to manage the camp for the full season. "Last Sunday we happily closed the twentieth year of operation, my fourth since being doomed to die of pernicious anemia three and a half years ago." He continued by telling Archbishop Mitty that he had experienced sixty-two blood transfusions, but that it had been eight weeks since his last transfusion, the longest period so far. He concluded his letter saying, "Sunshine Camp is also beneficial to second childhood." In a sermon at the camp he thanked the seminarian counselors for their blood donations. "These young men are giving me their blood and I am very grateful to them, but as Our Lord himself once said 'You cannot put new wine into old goat skins'." His business card at this time read, "Still alive at seventy-five on borrowed blood and borrowed time." Jim Flynn remembered Charlie holding a few funeral parties before his death. His attitude was that usually everyone except the deceased enjoys the party. "Why not celebrate your death before you die and participate."

Bill Cane and other seminarians took Charlie to Notre Dame Hospital, San Francisco, just before he died . At the camp he had tossed a stick at a dog and almost fell. "Oops, it's the beginning of the end," he remarked. "But that's all right." As they wheeled him down the hospital corridor in a chair, he began giving mock blessings like the Pope being carried on his special papal throne. When a very officious nurse with a serious face entered into his room to take his temperature, he pulled the thermometer out of his mouth and exclaimed, "Smile, damn you, smile!" The last words he uttered were "thank you." The date was July 18, 1958.

Charlie's Solemn Mass of Requiem was held at St. Mary's Church on Monday, July 21, 1958. The old brown gothic structure was packed with priests, former counselors, adult ex-campers, parishioners, and friends from his rural life battles. Rev. Thomas Farrell, Charlie's former associate from the 30's, celebrated the Mass, assisted by Fathers John Ralph Duggan, Donald McDonnell, John Garcia, Ronald Burke, and myself. Father John McCracken preached Charlie's eulogy. The Archdiocesan Priests Choir sang the Solemn Mass. McCracken's eulogy compared the life of a priest to a sermon and to the stained glass of a church window reflecting the qualities of Jesus. He spoke of Charlie's love of children, particularly his establishment of Sunshine Camp, his forty-seven years as a priest of the Archdiocese of San Francisco with fourteen of those years as Pastor of St. Mary's, his "classes" with the seminarian camp counselors where he would argue principles and practices in the hope that he might add something to their formation by sharing his experiences, and finally the acceptance of pain, suffering, and death which he humorously celebrated.

McCracken's eulogy ascended from the depth of his heart and friendship. He had lived with Charlie at St. Mary's, succeeded him at Sunshine Camp, and consulted with him often. His final words were, "It is proper that our last view of him is one clothed in the vestments of his priestly office. In a way he is now completing Mass, the mass that was his life, the Offertory of his life to God, the Consecration of his physical body in exchange for a spiritual one. And we pray that he may see God face to face, the God whom he reflected here on earth."

Charlie's body was finally interred in the priests' plot of St. Mary's Cemetery, Oakland, by another generation of Irish cemetery workers whose rights he had defended in years gone by. St. Mary's Parish had bought forty-seven acres, a portion of the A. Thomas Maloney's ranch for a cemetery in 1865. Charlie also joined seventy-five members of the Peralta family who are buried here, including the four Peralta sons who inherited the original land grant which included Oakland.

Charlie uttered many serious, humorous, and some very earthy phrases during his lifetime, all of which described his values, standards, and world view. Of all of his correspondence, talks, and messages, the following letter to Rev. Goldwin Moir, CSP of St. Mary's Church in Chinatown, San Francisco, best described Charlie. "You know I do not pretend to be a prophet, but I can see very closely that the only way to full Christianity is the way of the Catacombs and the catacomb spirit, to begin with in high places, and then all along the line a true spirit of simplicity, humility, humanity (truthfulness) and a spirit of poverty. If we begin all over from the Gospels and the Acts of The Apostles, skip Aristotle, and <u>The Thirteenth the Greatest of Centuries,</u> we can make a new start which Christ can bless."

During the McCarthy era, a Father George Dunne, S.J., a Jesuit priest involved in labor union issues, called a meeting at the University of San Francisco for all Catholic clergy and laity to discuss the issue of Communism and to let them know what the real story was. Dunne, seated at a table on a stage, had a large briefcase next to him which everyone could see.

Charlie stood in the rear of the hall walking from side to side during Dunne's presentation. Dunne remarked several times while pointing to his briefcase that it contained all of the names of and profiles of Bay Area subversives that they had been hearing about. Finally, after a third reference to the prominent briefcase, Charlie from the rear shouted "Bullshit!" and broke up the whole meeting.

According to Bishop John Cummins of the Diocese of Oakland, a former camp counselor and long time friend, Charlie fell in love with the French film <u>Monsieur Vincent</u>, the 1948 award winning and inspiring portrayal of the seventeenth century French priest Vincent de Paul who founded the Vincentian religious order of priests and the Daughters of Charity in the service of the poor. Charlie saw the film six times. Vincent's final words to his young novice Jeanne symbolized Charlie's whole life. Pierre Fresnay, playing Vincent, called Jeanne and said, "Remember always you'll find that charity is a heavy burden, heavier than the bowl of soup and the basket of bread. Giving bread and soup is not everything. The rich can do that. You are the little servant of the poor, the Maid of Charity, always smiling and good humored. They are your masters, fiercely exacting, you will see. The dirtier and uglier they are, the more vulgar and unjust, the more love you must show them. It is only because of your love, your love alone, that the poor will forgive you for the bread you give them."

Bill Cane, one of Charlie's camp counselors, wrote a chapter in a book of heroes who had influenced his life. "King of The Peasants" was a chapter about Charlie. Cane remembered a small Mexican boy coming up to him at Charlie's funeral with the question, "Will there be a camp now that Father Philipps is dead?" The question caused Cane to cry and respond, "Yes, certainly there will be a camp!" "The same question," continued Cane, "has echoed through my life. Will there be a camp? Will there be opportunities for minorities in America? Will there be health care for immigrant children? Will refugees be received? Will there be a just distribution of the world's goods? Will children the world over be able to eat and grow old and develop? Will we stop raping and poisoning the earth? When Chiapas blew up a few years ago and the Mexican government began killing the indigenous peasants, I didn't have to question whether we were doing the right thing taking the side of the peasants. The King of The Peasants was still out there in front, with the grim look and the glint in the eye. I was just following."

A few years ago I drove out to St. Mary's Cemetery to visit my mother's grave, and while there, inquired about the location of Charlie's. The cemetery has a special site for former priests perched on a small hilltop and marked with simple bronze plaques. I looked but could not locate Charlie's. However, I meditated there for awhile, remembering what a deep influence he made on my life and of many others. Here was a priest who "amused" so many children, rather than abusing them. I thanked him for that sense of justice which he instilled in my soul and which has continued to grow because of him. Like Bill Cane, whenever I am confronted with the injustices of society, Charlie's face looms up in front of me.

EPILOGUE

$\mathcal{W}$hile Charles Philipps developed a very innovative urban parish in the poor neighborhood of West Oakland, California, with a team of clergy, Holy Name Sister educators, Social Service Sisters, plus numerous volunteers who influenced and impacted the lives of families and children, he is better known, I think, for his rural social action activities. During his tenure as a rural pastor in Sebastopol, California, in the late 20's and as a spokesperson for the Catholic Rural Life Conference in the Archdiocese of San Francisco, he carried on a 20-year advocacy of rural social action. He defended small family farmers from the takeover by agribusiness and corporate agriculture. He was a loud proponent of the 160-acre limitation, which provided for the growth of family farming enterprises. He fought farm bankruptcies and bank foreclosures during the Depression. His support for farm worker organizing in Sonoma County made him many enemies, even among his farmer parishioners who also were unaware that he hid the union organizer in his rectory to avoid a sure tar and feathering. He took on the State Agricultural Department and helped to wrestle away their control of farm labor camps in California. His support and encouragement of farmer cooperatives led to the creation of apple co-ops in Sebastopol and grape co-ops in St. Helena and Windsor, California. He continued to urge farmers to form self help groups through his writings and radio addresses and tried to influence Stanford University and St. Mary's

College, Moraga, California, to develop courses in cooperatives within their Departments of Economics.

Charlie appeared and testified before State and Federal committees regarding a host of agricultural issues in California. He made countless speeches before civic and labor groups as well as gave radio talks on farming disputes. He supported rural electrification and community control of power and energy. He won the hearts of Portuguese dairy farmers in the San Joaquin Valley for his criticism of the State Agricultural Department's inspections of milk producers. He advocated for the Central Valley Project and spoke out against the efforts of private interests to control it.

Charlie authenticated Wendell Berry's image of an "agrarian" as a practice, an attitude, a loyalty, a passion, all based in a close connection with the land which begins with the love of fields and flows into good farming, good cooking, good eating, and gratitude to God. An early nutritionist he reigned at his seat in the rectory dining room surrounded by his jars of wheat germ, honey, and whole grain bread. He loved the taste of good cooking, especially his traditional Alsatian meals he took with his San Francisco Alsatian friends. He usually proceeded these with a tasty Manhattan accompanied by a good Napa Valley Zinfandel. Were he alive today he would join in with these crusading voices in the wilderness of rural America protesting and criticizing the influences of agribusiness and corporate farming and at the same time encouraging and supporting organic, sustainable, and wilderness farming. When Charlie railed against his ASSociated Farmers of America and their member large corporate farms in California in the 30's and 40's, he would bemoan the global spread of industrial agriculture in which seventy-five percent (75%) of agriculture's diversity during this past century has been lost.

The mind-set of corporate and industrial agriculture is one in which technology and seed industries aim to control seed worldwide, even to owning the property rights of its genetically engineered seed production. Where farmers for centuries saved and shared seeds for future plantings, industrial agriculture now legally forbids this time-honored custom and forces farmers to purchase expensive genetically developed seeds from a small number of monopolies. Where Charlie and his peasant father in Alsace fertilized and enriched their land naturally, corporate agriculture has introduced massive doses of pesticides into the world's farmlands. 20,000 farm workers suffer acute pesticide poisoning every year. The World Health Organization (WHO) in 1990 estimated that three million acute pesticide poisonings happen each year in developed countries, causing 220,000 deaths. Likewise, agricultural chemicals have entered the water runoffs of countless rivers and streams further poisoning fish and wildlife. 53 different pesticides applied to major food crops have been classified by the Federal Drug Administration (FDA) as "carcinogenic".

During his years as Catholic Rural Life Director, Charlie lamented the decline of family farms in California with the resulting loss of rural communities, cultures, and local business. Seventy years ago there were seven million American farmers. Today that number has dwindled to two million. From 1987 to 1992 the United States lost an average of 32,500 farms each year. The ASSociated Farmers of America in Charlie's time no longer dominate in California but have gone global with the purpose of determining what foods the world will eat while eliminating the diversity of foods of choice. Already in the past century industrial corporate agriculture has significantly decreased most of the lettuce, sweet corn, tomato, and asparagus diversity. Where local farm communities produced diversified crops, the result of global agriculture will be a monoculture of products.

One rural activist described the battles against worldwide-industrial agriculture like walking north through a line of railroad cars traveling south. Already an agrarian, cultural, and spiritual battle has emerged on the part of community supported-sustainable (small farms) agriculture, the organic food movement, together with new insights about food tastes, nutrition, and the growing awareness of the sacredness of the earth. Organic warriors, on the other hand, appear as the Davids against the Goliaths of industrial agriculture. Charlie would have applauded this development. Where originally viewed as something "hippie" and "fringe", the movement has become the fastest growing sector in U.S. agriculture and a competitor of industrial food. The local farmers' markets in urban cities are now a billion-dollar enterprise. More and more enlightened Americans are rallying for diversified and tasty food products. Slow Food, an international organization of 100 nations and 80,000 members, has dedicated its goal "to protect the pleasures of the table from the homogenization of modern fast food by promoting gastronomic culture, taste education, agricultural biodiversity from the dangers of extinction." Founded in 1986 Slow Food missionaries such as filmmaker Deborah Koons Garcia, wife of legendary Jerry Garcia, recently produced a 90 minute documentary "The Future of Food" about the dangers of genetically modified food. "If this technology isn't challenged and if this corporatization of our whole food system isn't stopped, at some point it will be too late," Garica stated in a San Francisco Chronicle November 7th, 2004, feature about the film.

The November 10th, 2004, edition of the Santa Rosa Press Democrat highlighted a growing movement of organic food at the Valley Vista Elementary School, Petaluma, California, where students plant, observe vegetable growth, pick, prepare, and cook garden organic products. They even learn composting the leftovers from their cafeteria. A School Garden Network of similar activities has begun in other Sonoma County, California, schools, educating and teaching young "fast food" addicts in the wonder of growing plants and the rich tastes of fresh produce. While the battle for "real" food wages between the "organics" and the industrialists, somebody needs to wake up the American public and educate them. As of 1997 forty-six percent of family food expenditures was spent on meals outside of the home, with thirty-four percent of the total food dollar spent on fast foods. As a corollary, from 1976 to 2000 obesity increased from 14 % to 30.9% of the U..S. population, causing Americans to spend about $30 billion each year on weight loss products and services. One needs only to study the supermarket check out counters to observe the "cooks" from the "eaters". "Cooks" will have a pile of fresh veggies, chicken, and fish, while the "eaters" will proudly exhibit their frozen pizzas, hash browns, and prepackaged meals. We need a food education revolution if the corporate and organic scales are going to be balanced.

"Today's industrial agriculture and large scale land holdings," wrote

Wendell Berry, "are neither inevitable nor likely to endure. Large scale can give way to small scale just as it has been done in the past, high tech to low tech. Corporate agriculture can yield to the reemergence of family enterprises. What comes around can go around."

The root difference between an industrial farmer and an organic one is basically their respective views of the earth. Industrial agriculture views nature as an enemy to be conquered and subdued, especially through the massive warfare of pesticides. The organic/agrarian mind is a spiritual and religious one which sees humanity as derived from the earth. The Roman Catholic rite of Ash Wednesday reminds believers to remember their association with nature. As the priest places the ashes on the forehead, he says, "Remember, man, that you are earth and into the earth you shall return."

The Earth is Mother Nature with all of her maternal qualities of life nurturing and caring. To the ancient Chinese she was a never depleted mammary gland embedded in the earth. Crops suckled her milk, and so did families. She was a never exhausted womb. Plant a seed, pray for fine weather, and she gave birth to the sustenance of life. To harm the earth is to insult one's ultimate mother.

The Book of Genesis describes the various days and stages of creation. God speaks to mankind and says, "See, I give you all the seed-bearing plants that are upon the whole earth and all the trees with seed-bearing fruit. This shall be your food. God saw all he had made and indeed it was very good."

Charles Philipps, priest, agrarian, and rural activist inherited his personal identity with the earth from his peasant father, when after tilling his soil with manure raked from his own barn, he cupped handfuls of earth to his nose and said, "It smells sweet."

OTHER SHEPHERDS—OTHER SHEEP

❦

$\mathcal{T}$he World War II military installations and war industries attracted Mexicans from the Southwest and Blacks from the South to West Oakland who replaced the ethnic Italians, Irish, and Greek families who moved out to East Oakland and San Leandro communities. The traditional ethnic atmosphere of the neighborhood was changing, housing stock decaying, and Oakland City politicians eyeing large blocks of West Oakland for a future freeway. Charlie could understand these changes and was able to adjust. He had been stationed at St. Mary's as an assistant pastor from 1918 to 1920 when West Oakland formed a vibrant middle class working peoples neighborhood. When he returned years later as Pastor from July 1936 to his retirement in 1950, he witnessed the slow flight of families and the gradual deterioration of the neighborhoods. Luckily for his parishioners and the city his personality and social awareness made it possible for him to adjust to these changes.

The traditional procedure whereby a priest was appointed to become a pastor of a selected parish was traditionally by seniority, the calendar date of his ordination. If a vacancy occurred at a parish through death or retirement, one could request an appointment to that particular parish based on the fact that his ordination class was next in line. The individual priest may not have received an immediate appointment, but at least he felt that he was certain to receive one in the near future. According to this custom there was no attempt by the local bishop or his administration to fit the man to the neighborhood, the culture, and certainly not to a local language. The Church had one concept of community which was the parish community of families and individuals for whom the parish staff provided the liturgies, religious services, and educational programs primarily for the spiritual benefit and religious safeguard of its people. Catholics in San Francisco and Chicago identified themselves not by their neighborhoods (the Mission, Noe Valley, or the Richmond), but rather by their parishes. One was from Saint Anne's, Mission Dolores, or St. Peter and Paul. Chicagoans were from Resurrection (Westside) and Presentation (Southside). My Chicago friend, J.R. Collins, remembers his mother saying at the dinner table, "Pass the mashed potatoes down to this end of the parish." Only in recent times did the concept of a parish as an integral chip in the mosaic of a neighborhood begin to emerge. Tom Brokaw, in his book <u>A Long Way From Home: Growing Up in the American Heartland in the Forties and Fifties,</u> described the effect of the White flight to America's suburbs following World War II. Where previously neighborhood and parish had a strong identity mark, Brokow observed, " There was no more corner to hang out in."

The appointments of the three pastors following Charlie's retirement and death, namely John Walsh, Alvin Wagner, and Joseph Pier, were based not on their capacity to understand and relate to the neighborhood, especially a poverty one such as West Oakland. All three were traditionally educated to be shepherds of a parish flock. None of them had any sensitivity or understanding of poverty or social justice issues. Charlie, on the other hand, saw himself not only as a shepherd but because of his sense of justice, he was comfortable with the poor and directed his troops to serve the whole community. John Walsh tried in his own way, Wagner ignored it, and Pier ran Charlie's spirit into the ground.

THE JOLLY TINKER

꿰Ⓞ꿰

*I*rishman John Walsh from Thurles, Ireland, was a physically huge man with a large head of silver white hair combed straight back, big nose, ruddy face marked by two deep channels running from his eye lids down his cheeks, and large fleshy hands and feet. In fact his nickname among his Irish clergy friends was "Shoes Walsh". Everything about him was extra large. He came to Oakland from Escalon, a small rural parish in Stanislaus County. St. Mary's was his first assignment as a city pastor. The Archbishop made a clean sweep of St. Mary's clergy by reassigning John Duggan and Luis Almendares and appointing Walsh, Ray Thomas, and myself. Ray and I showed up on Saturday as our letter of appointment directed. Walsh arrived later that week. The Archbishop's office thought that I was fluent in Spanish and could replace Duggan and Almendares, both fluent Spanish speakers. I could speak some Spanish, but certainly wasn't skilled enough to preach, understand what sins people rattled off in confessional, or counsel people with personal problems. So I learned my Spanish "on the street" and experienced many embarrassing moments. Once in a sermon I made several references to the Pope and Holy Father as "La Papa" and "La Santa Papa". I didn't understand why the congregation was smiling and laughing until I was told that I called the Pope "The Potato" and worse, "The Holy Potato". Another time I suggested flipping a coin with Eduardo, a heavy set Mexican gentleman who ran a small café down on 7th Street where a young teen-age boy and I went for coffee. Eduardo wanted to give me the coffee free, but I suggested that we flip for it. In Mexico one chooses "sol" (sun) or "aguila" (eagle) in a coin toss. Not knowing this I came up with my Spanish version of heads and tails, which came out as "heads" or "ass hole" in front of everyone in the café. Eduardo turned red as a tomato and two young Mexicans laughingly spit out their coffee on the counter, while my wide-eyed friend regarded me with wonder and shock. As we left the café, he remarked, "Padre, you say some bad words in there." I did learn the difference between "tail" (cola) and "ass hole" (culo). Another time in the confessional, an elderly Mexican lady asked me if she was obligated by the Lenten regulation for fasting, eating only one meal a day. She used the word "ajunar" (to fast), which sounded to my poorly trained ear very similar to "orinar" (to pee), which word I did know. Knowing that Lent was a forty day affair, I suggested she ask me the next day, which would give me time to find out what she was talking about.

John Walsh belonged to that group of Irish clergy of the 30's and 40's who crowded the various seminaries of Ireland and were adopted by American bishops to serve in their dioceses. Since the Irish church could not absorb them, students found assignments in foreign English speaking countries of England, Scotland, Australia, New Zealand, and the United States. From the 1920's to 1940's Irish born clergy or "FBI's" (Foreign Born Irish) significantly augmented local American clergy and made up the majority of the clergy in some parts of the U.S.A. Bidding wars, like art auctions, went on in Irish seminaries by visiting American bishops or their representatives with offers of annual paid vacation home, personal autos, and other enticements, it these young seminarians would choose their diocese. Soon the news of American "deals" quickly propagated in the theology schools of the Emerald Isle.

Walsh socially identified with a group of five Irish priests who enjoyed golf, horses, good food, bourbon, and poker. Monday was a "holy day of obligation" when they golfed at Sequoia Country Club, Oakland, and where clergy received free privileges. His group took turns hosting dinner at their rectories, while American clergy frequented San Francisco restaurants. Each host would try to out do the others with the dinner menu. The dinner usually featured a large roast beef surrounded with roasted potatoes, onions, and carrots or a combination of roasted chicken and ham. Frequently the guests would needle each other, share the latest clerical gossip, and flatter the cook with such Irish blarney as, "Ah, Mary, the roast was as tender as a maiden's heart!" Following dinner the group would proceed to the host's study for a game of cards. One famous game included Walsh and the San Francisco auxiliary bishop at the time, Thomas J. Connolly, who later became the Archbishop of Seattle, Washington.

Connolly was a fierce competitor with an equally vicious temper. When he played his cards on the table and began to rake in the pot, Walsh respectfully interrupted him with "excuse me Bishop, but I believe I won this hand!", which he had. In a rage, Connolly hurled his cards at Walsh exclaiming, "you sonofabitch!" Walsh, with his huge fingers slowly gathering the pot to his chest, softly muttered, "Ah Bishop, I've been called many names in my lifetime, but this is the first time a sonofabitch by a bishop." He and Connolly had a humorous run-in years before when Walsh was a young curate at St. Charles' Parish, San Francisco, and Connolly was the pastor of Mission Dolores in the Mission District. Walsh leveled a formal protest against a Mission Dolores basketball team in the Catholic Parish league for playing an illegal player who happened to be an excellent player but also Jewish. In those days participants in the Catholic Youth Organization (CYO) had to present a valid baptismal certificate to qualify. Connolly called Walsh roaring over the phone, "Who do you think you are protesting this game?" Walsh referred to the Jewish boy by name, and Connolly shot back, "How do you know?" Walsh replied, "Because he played for us last year!"

Walsh's most outstanding trait was his dedication and enjoyment of fellow priests, whoever they were. He would welcome priest strangers into his house for as long as they wished to stay and reached out to those with problems, particularly alcoholics. One day he asked me to drive to San Francisco's Tenderloin district to pick up an Irish priest with a long history of alcoholism and bring him back to St. Mary's. "Remember," said Walsh, "He's Mr. Ryan, when you call for him at the hotel." Sober and alert, Mr. Ryan began to sermonize as we headed over the Bay Bridge, "Now, young fellow, learn a lesson from me. Watch out for the booze!" Then he began to relate that while he'd been a long term alcoholic, "I never laid hands on a woman in my life!" Walsh was not home when we arrived at the parish house, so I escorted him to the pastor's study and left him there. Unfortunately, his seat on the couch gave him a direct view of Walsh's liquor cabinet. He was dead drunk by the time Walsh came home.

Gregarious, humorous, and compassionate, John would turn on his Irish charm in trying to get an irate husband to talk about his troubled marriage. "You know," he would start, "You don't sound as bad as you wife described you," and soon he'd have the person eating out of his hand and agreeing to a meeting. He was pleasant and cooperative to the school nuns and the Social Service Sisters, leaving them alone and giving them anything they needed. Respectful and paternal to me, he allowed me complete control over the Spanish speaking community. Concerned about the spiritual needs of his people, he invited visiting clergy to conduct retreats and novenas both in Spanish and English. After being impressed by a new sound system at St. Leo's Church, Piedmont, he directed me to contact Nick Connolly, the pastor and obtain the name of the company that had installed it. For John a sound system was a microphone and a pair of large speakers. The sound company, however, was a group of sound engineers who needed to test the acoustics of the church late at night when there was little auto traffic outside. Seeing the lights on at 11 p.m., Walsh instructed me to tell the engineers to leave. The first Sunday we used the new system, I noticed Walsh slowly walking back and forth across the rear of the church during my sermon. "That's a great system," he exclaimed after the Mass. "I could hear you very clearly!" I didn't have it in me to tell him that I had forgotten to turn it on.

One day he decided that he really didn't know his parishioners and went out into the neighborhood knocking on doors to introduce himself. After the tenth house of all Spanish-speaking families, he retreated back to the rectory beaten and defeated. "Shit," he said, "Here I am the Pastor and I can't even communicate with the people!"

Like a true Irishman, Walsh had a love for horses. Every so often he would just disappear for three or four days without telling anybody. He would visit an Irish priest friend who lived near the Del Mar racetrack in Southern California. Walsh would stay with him, borrow his car, and attend the races. One time following the last race, he came out to the parking lot and could not remember what the car looked like. So he hailed a cab, retreated to the nearest bar, and after two hours, returned to see a lone car in the lot. He tried the key and presto he was off.

During his two years at St. Mary's, Walsh was consistently kind and attentive to Charlie. Both had been stationed in the country, had mutual friends, and could share stories. In June 1952 "Shoes" went walking to St. Anthony's Parish in East Oakland and after several years to St. James Church in San Francisco. He later retired to Ireland where clerical gossip described him as sad and depressed over the changes in the Church, particularly the large number of men leaving the active priesthood. He once recounted his first experience of seeing a revolving door with another Irish priest as they witnessed the merry-go-round horde of bodies entering and exiting at the same time. "Ah, Mike," said Walsh, "To think we cried when we left the old country!" John had lost his sense of humor, his joviality, and his gregariousness. His clerical world and his personal church had disappeared. Not able to cope with the changes, he returned to Ireland to retire and die.

THE RINGMASTER

⚮

*C*harlie's next successor after Walsh was Alvin P. Wagner, whose appointment had an interesting political twist. Wagner had been a 15-year member of the Archdiocesan Mission Band, a group of four priests who toured the Archdiocese of San Francisco, preaching week-long retreats, novenas, and missions for the spiritual motivation of the people. Wagner was also the founder of the Rosary Hour, which organized local priests and parishioners to recite the rosary over local radio stations throughout the Archdiocese. He was first offered the pastorship of St. Anthony's in East Oakland, which he declined and asked for a more prestigious one in San Francisco, which was "open" for a pastor. Wagner's reaction so infuriated Archbishop Mitty at the time that he appointed Wagner to the poverty–minority neighborhood of St. Mary's. Socially one couldn't go any lower than St. Mary's. A few more blocks down and you would fall into the Oakland Estuary.

Wagner by experience and temperament was completely unfit and incapable of directing a parish like St. Mary's. Personally, he was the opposite of most priests and men of his time. He didn't drink, smoke, enjoy sports, or host friends. He was the kind that you would put in right field where he couldn't do too much damage to the team. In Al's case, this wouldn't work out because he couldn't catch. He was interested in Church gossip and clerical history, which he enjoyed sharing with Charlie. Other than sharing a physical location of the church buildings and house, there was little else one could share with Wagner. Where he lacked any intellectual depth, he made up for with emotion. He was constantly excited about some new and different project, which he assumed would also make you enthusiastic as well. While he might have been initially hurt by Mitty's assignment, he arrived at 7th and Jefferson Streets and immediately took off like a rocket.

Al's view of St. Mary's was a circus tent of empty stands, which he as the Ringmaster would fill up through the sensational acts he would dream up. For the next two years, Wagner became the ecclesiastical Barnum and Bailey of West Oakland. His potential audience didn't live in the run down parish neighborhood. He envisioned hordes of spiritually hungry souls rushing out of the Oakland hills and through the Caldecott Tunnel from wealthy Contra Costa County.

Life with Al was one hectic moment after another. Fortunately for me, he wasn't interested in the Mexicans, Black and low-income seniors, and left me alone to work with them. It wasn't that he did not like them, he was really incapable of understanding and relating to them. So he set out to make St. Mary's a "devotional" church, promoting every imaginable pietistic activity that might draw outside people. He fantasized St. Mary's in the same mode as San Francisco's St. Patrick's Church and Old St. Mary's, Chinatown, on the edge of the wealthy business community. The only difference was that St. Mary's was in West Oakland, old, run down, dirty, and not the neighborhood where you would park your car to attend evening services.

His first event was a novena in honor of Our Lady of Lourdes. The church had a long established grotto with a statue of the Virgin Mary resembling that of the famous miracle shrine in France. The shrine, by the way, also featured three two inch pipes capped with a slot for offerings which would descend into a box in the basement of the church. Charlie had designed these years ago because of vandalism to the candelabra and the poor boxes. However, he had forgotten to tell us about these, so that when we discovered them six months later, we took out about $600 in coins. Al proceeded to advertise the novena in the East Bay press with the enticing offer of "Free Holy Water from Lourdes" at the concluding service. People were invited to participate for nine days and then would receive a vial of miraculous water. He actually had a pint of water from the French shrine which he mixed with a few gallons of East Bay municipal water, filling several hundred vials for the final service. I questioned him of the reality of the mixture, but in his mind the French molecules met their Oakland cousins, embraced, and transferred their miracle making power.

The final evening of the novena became a zoo scene. According to the tradition of the Catholic Church, whenever you give away anything like ashes on Ash Wednesday, palms on Palm Sunday, or bless animals on St. Francis Day, you can be assured of a crowd. The novena's last night was no exception. Al had set up three tables in the church's vestibule staffed by volunteers who would pass out one vial per person. No sooner had the final hymn concluded when the hordes of worshipers crashed through the doors like a crowd of Mexican children at the bursting of a piñata, grabbing handfuls of holy water vials and pushing the volunteers aside. Al was running around screaming, "Only one to each person!" He almost said "customer!" The faithful were not satisfied with a mere four ounces; they were going for a pint!

Al's next production was a novena honoring the Holy Souls. He concluded that since everyone had some favorite friend or relative who had died, all kinds of people would stream down to St. Mary's to honor their deceased loved ones. Al didn't realize that while Catholics might attend a service on one day like All Souls Day or the Mexican Day of the Dead, most people wouldn't come for nine days. One of his references for success was that only in the San Francisco Convent of the Helpers of the Holy Souls was there a novena of this kind. Unfazed and brimming with enthusiasm, he proceeded with plans for three daily services: 9 a.m. for retired folk, 12 noon for the downtown business crowd, and 7:30 p.m. for anyone else. He asked me to request the loan of a casket from my mortician father, which would be covered in black to simulate a funeral service. My father thought the whole idea was crazy and declined loaning one for nine days in case he could sell it. So Al put three card tables together, covered them in black cloth, and held a mock funeral Mass every morning, sprinkling them with holy water and incense, as in an actual funeral service. Bill Hennebry, an Irish priest appointed in Walsh's time, exclaimed to me at breakfast after one of these

Masses, "Jesus, I've been a priest for forty years, and this is the first time I've ever incensed a card table!" Needless to say, the Holy Souls Novena was a complete flop. Nobody but a few neighborhood souls came to witness this strange event. Looking down at the 500-seat church from the elevated pulpit was like sitting high above home plate, looking at the attendance of two last place teams.

Al's failed novena didn't seem to damper his enthusiasm. He didn't talk about it and went right on to his next "show", a Southern Barbecue cooked by a black parishioner with a secret barbecue sauce. Al wasn't having too much luck with outside attendance, so he looked to the neighborhood, picturing hordes of people walking around the school yard with heaping plates of barbecue and potato salad. Since he didn't have a barbecue pit, he went ahead and had one built, a ten-foot long concrete pit with metal grates that cost $1,500. In his mind this first barbecue would lead into a tradition and would repay the costs of the pit. "Barbecue Sunday" came and like the novena, few customers showed up. Finally, the black chef, now very discouraged, asked what he was supposed to do with forty pounds of chicken. We were all so tired that we put it all, unwrapped, into the freezer. The next day we witnessed this huge block of frozen chicken parts all stuck together. I leaned into the freezer with a hammer and screwdriver trying to separate the frozen mess. Legs, wings, pieces of breast, came flying off like wood chips from a logger's axe. Finally, I realized how ridiculous this whole saga was from start to finish, put the chicken igloo into my car, and delivered it to the local Catholic Worker soup kitchen. The neighborhood homeless feasted for days.

Convinced that he had to improve the financial state of the parish, Al next embarked on a carnival that also featured gambling. He had a contact with the manager of the local Moose Lodge, where members illegally gambled behind closed doors. Al borrowed crap tables, Blackjack, and other games of chance, turning the upstairs auditorium into a casino. A croupier from the Moose Club also came along to run the games. Friday and Saturday night people crowded around and, enticed by the frenzy of winning, bet heavily. Al was ecstatic, smiling, patting people on the back with his eyes full of dollar signs. While he and the crowds were watching the dice roll up and down the table, Tillio Fazio, a long time parishioner with a sharp eye, was observing the guest dealer pocketing cash with his assistant girl friend. Fazio relayed his suspicions to Al who called the Moose manager to come and observe the dealer. This was on Sunday afternoon, the last day of the carnival. He confirmed the theft and immediately replaced the dealer. No one could estimate how much was stolen.

Al the optimist kept rolling along. His plans for an Easter Sunday Solemn High Mass included members of the San Francisco Symphony and Chorus. He bought extensive advertisements in East Bay newspapers, wrote press releases, and bought new gold vestments. Easter Sunday morning every seat and aisle was packed with a crown that spilled out onto the front stairs. Al was emotionally drunk with excitement as he bounded into the sacristy and began to put on the new vestments while Bill Hennebry and I stood by ready to accompany him on his triumphal entry into the sanctuary. No one, however, had anticipated Maria Munoz, "Blind Mary" as we called her, a very eccentric Mexican lady who pretended to be blind, carried a red and white cane, and hit the end of the pews as she made her daily walk up the church aisle. When the Symphony Chorus proceeded to blow the ceiling into space with a pre-Mass Alleluia, Maria, seated in the front pew, jumped up and started screaming, "Stop that music!" Next the janitor ran into the sacristy and yelled, "Father Wagner, that blind Mexican woman is screaming!" You could hear Maria loud and clear. Al ripped off his vestments, rushed out to the church, and literally dragged Maria out of her seat in front of everyone, and pushed her out of the church. No one was going to wreck his show!

When Al did "liturgy" he would go into his piety position, head folded slowly to the side like on a pillow, a tight-lipped mouth, and his shoulders hunched over. Once during a procession he held the ornate gold monstrance, with a large Eucharistic host in a glass case. In front of him walked six little flower girls with their white veils and billowy dresses. Each one carried a basketful of rose petals. The procession stopped at each corner of the church with the girls turning toward Al, throwing their petals, and in one loud voice chanted in exaggerated slow tones, "Adoration, Supplication, Thanksgiving, and Praise to Our Lord and Savior (stop, take a breath and go) Jesus Christ in the Most Blessed Sacrament of the altar." By the time the fifth exclamation happened I was ready to explode. In my mind, I blamed the school nuns for this demonstration. Afterwards, I questioned Al, "What nun thought up that ridiculous chant?" And he slowly replied, "That was my idea."

His final spectacle at St. Mary's was the creation and erection of an outdoor marble shrine to Our Lady of Fatima on the Eighth Street garden alongside the church. Al's strategy was to erect a shrine, which would attract the sizeable Portuguese community of the East Bay. He imagined hundreds of Portuguese pilgrims like the medieval and modern day ones, who make the "Camino", traversing the Pyrenees to the shrine of Compostella in Northern Spain. Here they would pass through Hayward, San Leandro, and East Oakland. Al ordered the marble statuary from Italy and erected a red brick platform on which he placed Our Lady of Fatima with admiring children and sheep in the garden below looking up in wonder. He had been planning his spectacle for months. Eighth Street from Broadway to Jefferson would be blocked off while a procession of Portuguese religious societies with their banners held aloft would solemnly march to the shrine for the solemn consecration by the Archbishop and brightly vested clergy. The event was planned for a late summer date. But disaster struck through a June letter from the Archbishop assigning him to St. Francis Assisi Church in San Francisco's North Beach.

So the Ringmaster folded up his tents and paraded out of Oakland, crossed the Bay Bridge, and reopened his show in the midst of the hippies, coffeehouses, and the skin shows of Broadway, San Francisco. Not to be outdone by the neighborhood dazzle, he convinced a wealthy woman patron to buy and ship the statue of St. Francis created by the famous and eccentric Benny Bufano. The statue was gathering dust in a Paris warehouse. Al had it erected on the outside stairs of St. Francis Church. He also fixed a brass plate at the base, which recognized the generosity of his patron. Buffano became infuriated at the desecration of his work. The San Francisco press described Buffano one night banging away with hammer and chisel, Al's calling the cops, and a standing-room-only of Saturday night North Beach revelers.

Al ended his days in Alameda, California, as pastor of St. Joseph's Church. Not content with just a church, he worked some church politics to have it elevated to the status of a Basilica so that it became "The Basilica of St. Joseph", like some of the famous Roman Basilicas. He died there at his Basilica, but not before one of his associate priests tried to burn it down.

REVEREND SCROOGE

⌒◠◯◠⌒

If John Walsh was the Jolly Tinker, and Alvin Wagner, JT Barnum, then Joseph Mary Pier, the third pastor with whom Charlie spent his retirement, could be classified as the Reverend Abeneezer Scrooge. Born March 15, 1893, in Coerfeld, Westphalia, Germany, he entered the Minor Seminary of St. Joseph's College, Mt. View, California, as an older student (32) and was ordained a priest for the Archdiocese of San Francisco on June 20, 1931. Following his ordination, he served in short-time assignments in both rural and urban parishes of the Archdiocese. He arrived as Pastor of St. Mary's, Oakland, in June of 1954.

A small statured man of about five feet three inches tall, he wore a crown of gray hair around a bald pate, which was frequently topped by a black pleated electrician's cap. A small round face and nose was pinched by wire-rimmed glasses. Soon after his arrival, the relaxed air of John Walsh and the animated dervishness of Al Wagner gave way to the gloom and pettiness of Joe Pier.

He seemed a lonely man who had no visible friends among the clergy. Perhaps because he was older than his contemporary seminary students and came from a different background, he didn't make for deep friendships or camaraderie. No priest friends ever came to visit or have dinner. He would faithfully take his day off, but rarely tell what he did. I had also heard that in earlier times he would spend his three-week summer vacations substituting for other priests at their parishes and receiving an additional salary. His relationships with his assistant priests were cold and controlling. Talk at the dinner table was strained and feigned. Prior to his arrival, both assistant priests took responsibility for covering incoming phone and office calls. If one had to go somewhere, the other covered for him. Joe, however, didn't accept this arrangement and insisted that you take "duty" for the entire week. Essentially, you were under house arrest and Joe's eyes during your week "on duty". Father Leo Uglesic, a Croatian priest who escaped the Tito regime in Yugoslavia, had emigrated to Argentina with his family, came to the Bay Area, and was assigned to St. Mary's with me. St. Mary's was a very busy place. Street people rang the doorbell day and night. The parish office was like a Bureau of Births and Deaths. As the oldest Catholic church in Oakland, people were constantly requesting baptismal certificates in order to receive their Social Security benefits. One day before Joe's edict about weekly "duty," I asked Leo to cover for me while I went out for a haircut. Returning to my room upstairs I was soon confronted by Joe who asked me where I had been in the past two hours. After explaining that Leo had covered for me, he responded briskly, "Get your haircut on your week off duty!" Father Ron Burke who took my place after I left for Social Work School at the Catholic University of America, Washington D.C., had a similar experience with Joe who also confronted him for being gone from the rectory. Burke explained that he had gone to see his spiritual director and had gone to confession. Pier's response was "You went to confession last week."

Even though the parish finances were at an all time low during Joe's pastorship, he evidenced all the personal features of a "tightwad". For example, when he replaced a burned out light bulb, he would write the date of the replacement on the bulb. When these burned out prior to their guaranteed expiration date, he would send it back to the manufacturer and request a new one. Joe also controlled the parish checkbook by personally doing the grocery shopping at the nearby Housewives Market, a block long historic Oakland food emporium. He also instructed the cook to save all the leftovers, especially meat, all of which would end up in a personally designed stew served at the end of the week featuring all the parts and pieces of leftovers of previous meals. What a far cry from the roast beef and chicken with bacon of the Walsh years! Charlie, a usual evening meal participant, quickly discovered the decline in the quality of the cuisine and soon took himself to the homes of friends. The cook usually had a bowl of fresh fruit on the dining room table. One afternoon I took an apple and, walking upstairs, met Joe who spied the apple and blurted out, "What are you doing? That fruit is for meals!"

Joe, after saying his morning Mass and finishing his breakfast, would spend most of his time with a pair of pliers and screwdriver in his hands repairing windows, doors, and other parts of the parish buildings. One day, dressed in my black clerical suit and Roman collar, I opened the tabernacle on the church altar and extracted communion hosts to take to a house bound senior. Joe was repairing something in the adjoining sacristy. He came out and seeing the open tabernacle, fell immediately to his knees and began to shake his head back and forth muttering "tsk, tsk, tsk" to show his displeasure that I was not garbed in a soutane and white surplice. That did it for me! All of my repressed anger and annoyance exploded as I turned to him and shouted, "SHUT UP!" That incident, as with many others, would be followed by notes from Joe on torn pieces of paper in which he would refer to the Canon Law on taking communion to the sick or whatever. Joe couldn't confront a person face to face, but left these little love notes at the bottom of the stairs where you were sure to see them. Ron Burke saved a whole collection of "Peirisms", the most famous one was "Stop feeding the Bums!", a reference to Burke's raiding the refrigerator to give food to a hungry person at the front door.

Pier spent four years at St. Mary's before he was transferred out of the Oakland ghetto of West Oakland to the fast growing suburban community of Pleasanton, California, where probably skimping and scrounging were not his preoccupation anymore. He served as pastor of St. Augustine's Church from 1959 to 1965 when he retired due to ill health. In a letter to Bishop Floyd Begin of the Oakland Diocese, he described his ten years suffering from phlebitis in his legs, which was very painful and deprived him of sleep. He spent his last years in a Franciscan retirement home in San Antonio, Texas, where he passed away at age 78 on June 15, 1971. He is buried in St. Augustine's parish cemetery, Pleasanton, California.

THE REVENGE OF THE RADICAL PEASANT

❦

$\mathcal{I}$ have often thought about how my social conscience, world view, and personality would have been formed had I been appointed to an upper class parish neighborhood in Marin or San Mateo counties where the majority of the people were white, Anglo, affluent, and most probably conservative Republicans.

On the other hand, West Oakland in the 1950's, St. Mary's Parish, and my five years association with Charlie Philipps had a definite impact on my world view, my social conscience, and my personal desire to do what I could to develop a level playing field in Oakland. I witnessed a decaying neighborhood, skid row drunks ringing the doorbell in the middle of the night, the early birth of heroin use and its effects on young adults, one of whom, Sam Aguirre, got his throat slashed in a drug deal gone bad. I remember Officer Joe Taylor of the Oakland Police Department asking me to intervene with the mother of one of our school children who had taken over her husband's drug business while he served time. Taylor did not want to arrest her but to get her to identify her supplier. A very surprised and embarrassed lady she was when I arranged an interview with her in the parish office.

Being called out often to minister to elderly pensioners living in old transient hotel rooms, many of them alcoholics in one room with a hot plate, taught me the loneliness of old age and the effort to beautify their drab surroundings.

One late night I drove into the carport to hear a low moan coming from the other side. There I found Larry on a heap of water hoses completely "soused". Larry attended Mass every morning, but when he failed to show up after a few days, I knew he was on a bender.

Margaret, for example, personified the multitudinous types of characters in our cities' ghettos who are "down in their luck," yet struggle to maintain a sense of dignity. In Margaret's case whenever there was a large church event, Margaret would feign a heart attack solely to get attention. All one had to say was "Call an ambulance" and Margaret would be up on her feet completely healthy. Following the morning mass she would daily tour the church stopping at every saint's statue, lighting a candle, and saying a prayer. She was also a member of the Ladies of Mercy Sodality, an ancient parish organization that was down to three members. During John Walsh's pastorship she and her other members were assigned the linen booth of the parish bazaar in the upstairs auditorium. Some one had donated an Irish linen table cloth and twelve napkins which Margaret assumed would land in her booth. However, it was decided to do a special raffle rather than have some one win it for a twenty-five cent bet. Margaret was furious and started to bawl when informed of the decision. I was asked to go over to her booth and console her. When I asked her what was the matter, she responded, "Nobody gives a shit for the Ladies of Mercy!"

Besides having a significant Mexican population and elderly pensioners, St. Mary's also had a small group of Black Catholics who had a men's organization called the Knights of St. Peter Claver. Once a year a small group of men would assemble with their capes, swords, and funny Napoleanic hats, and march down the main aisle. Black Catholics at this time were not allowed membership in the well known Catholic men's organization, the Knights of Columbus, so they organized their own fraternal group in honor of the famous Black saint of Peru.

Too, the early morning file of down and out men waiting for coffee and a piece of bread served by the Social Service Sisters, the sisters loading up their station wagon full of food to deliver to poor families, their celebrations of Las Posadas in the Social Hall for hundreds of kids and their families.

The ex-con whom I helped get a Greyhound bus ticket to see "his poor mother" in Southern California, stealing my golf clubs out of my car and trying to "pawn" them at a Broadway Street pawn shop, the owner calling the police, my reporting the theft and being told that the clubs were at the Central Police station in the City Hall, and I in my clerical suit and Roman collar walking out of City Hall at noon, the clubs slung over my shoulder with passers–by ribbing me about playing golf that day. Later that evening my thief calling me from the City Hall jail telling me that the court was going to give him 60 days for stealing my clubs and "I was the only one who could help him."

My innocent eyes were weekly opened wide to the world of crime in my visits to the Oakland City Jail, the Alameda County Jail, and the Alameda County Juvenile Hall, all of which were located within the boundaries of St. Mary's. John Duggan was responsible for starting weekly visits to the jails which I assumed after his transfer. I had never been in a jail in my life nor spoken to a criminal or a teen age delinquent. As I toured cell blocks, I was welcomed by most inmates, made friends with them, and left the jails with a laundry list of wives and girl friends to call. On my first walk through the girls' section of the Juvenile Hall, I was "wolf whistled" at which was a first to me. I heard confessions for those who needed to unload their guilt. I still remember the very pleasant looking teen age boy who had calmly shot and killed his parents as they watched TV. I said Mass on Christmas Eve in the City Jail which was a "first" for them. All in all, the jail staff were a friendly group who welcomed my visits.

Evelio Grillo, a Black Cuban American, has been a deep friend and mentor from my St. Mary's days. Grillo as Director of the Alexander Community Center in West Oakland worked very closely with Father John Duggan and their "at risk" Mexican boys. Duggan started the St. Mary's Boys Club, dug out the basement of the school, created a boxing ring, and recruited some ex-fighters like Jimmy Delgadillo ("Baby Tarzan") and Gene Ronstat to train these future champions The whole St. Mary's neighborhood used to turn out for these Friday night fight cards.

Grillo used to borrow Duggan's Jeep station wagon to do his family's grocery shopping. One Saturday he arrived late to discover that Duggan was out in the church hearing confessions. He encountered a line of penitents waiting to confess so he got in line. Grillo had been raised a Catholic as a child in a Tampa, Florida, neighborhood (Yorba City) of Black Cubans, but was no longer a practicing Catholic. Finally, when his time came to enter the confessional, he knelt down and exclaimed "Pappy Duggan! It's me, Grillo. Don't get excited! All I want is the keys to the Jeep!"

Later on Duggan made a permanent gift of keys and Jeep to Grillo's family. Grillo taught me so much about working with minority families and kids, essentially that they had to feel your love for them. He left West Oakland as a Fellowship Recipient to attend the University of California, Berkeley School of Social Work, became a successful group work leader for the Oakland Recreational Department, as well as the Guru for aspiring Black political leaders in Oakland. Now retired at 85 he lives at a 10th and Jefferson Street apartment, three blocks from St. Mary's. We recently celebrated our 55 years of friendship. He calls me "Brother". We are.

My friendship with Cesar Chavez started at St. Mary's where Fred Ross, Sr., the famous community organizer directed Cesar to ask me to help him organize his first house meeting. Cesar was being trained as an Organizer for the Community Service Organization (CSO), the early effort of Sol Alinsky to develop political power in Spanish Speaking communities. My friendship with Cesar continued as he went forward to organize the United Farm Workers and sought my help in various boycott efforts of the union.

I have often wondered whatever happened to Marta, a plumpish 37 year old Mexican woman with three children, all from different fathers. Loud, aggressive, and demanding, she appeared at the rectory office one day insisting that we give her money for her children. Since the children were all born in the United States, they qualified for Family Assistance which included rent, food, and clothing. Marta didn't know how to make her welfare check last through the month. After paying her rent, she would buy everything by the case: milk, canned goods, bread.

By the middle of the month she was broke, and that's when she would be ringing the door bell. She usually came as we priests were finishing our evening meal. One evening seated in the waiting room, she heard us exiting the dining room and with a very loud voice she shouted through the wall, "Father Cox, I know you are there!" I had no doubt as to whom the voice belonged.

Marta was the best known illegal immigrant in the East Bay. She would be picked up frequently by the Immigration and Naturalization Service (INS), put on a bus, and dropped off at the Tijuana border. However, Marta was extremely intelligent and resourceful. She would beg outside of Tijuana churches until she had enough money to cross over and be back in Oakland.

One day she informed me that the INS had told her that she better get out of Oakland or else she would be picked up again. We discussed several cities where she might not be known. "Fresno?" I asked. "No! They know me there." I listed several other places in California where she would not be recognized, but she repeated her "No's". Finally, I asked if she had ever been to Sacramento. She replied "no," so immediately I leapt to the realization that Sacramento would be my escape from Marta. I told her that I would help her get there and also provide her with the name of a priest friend of mine. Marta and her children left on a bus for Sacramento. A few days later I received an irate call from my priest friend saying, "What in the hell are you doing to me?" I replied "Friend, we both belong to the Catholic, Universal Church. I have had Marta for over a year. Now she is yours. Bless you!"

My seminary training did not include a workshop on how one administers a pledge to stop drinking alcohol until one day an older Irishman accompanied by a younger man rang the doorbell and asked to see a priest who was on duty that day, so I entered the waiting room, introduced myself, and asked how I could help them. The younger man spoke first, describing himself as a bartender at a local saloon, and introduced the older man who wanted to take the pledge. He also explained that his friend under the promise of a pledge would honor it religiously.

I had absolutely no idea of how to administer a pledge, so I excused myself, went upstairs to John Walsh, the pastor, and asked him. "Oh, just write some kind of a promise on parish letterhead and have him sign it." So looking very officious I reentered the office, paper and pen in hand, and began to write out a promise. " How long do you want to take this for?" I inquired. "For life!" he answered. "I always take it for life." So I wrote "for life", handed him the paper, and said "sign here". He regarded me with a question mark and a disdainful face and with paper in hand exclaimed, "What in the hell is this?" "I haven't promised you one damned thing". Then he turned to the young bartender and stated "Will you look at this! These priests study for 10 to 12 years and they don't even know how to give a pledge!"

Next, he looked at me and said, "You have to get me down on my knees with my hands on the Bible and make me swear out loud!" At this point I was both embarrassed and angry that this old drunk had shown me up, so I got out the largest Bible I could find, put both his hands inside of it, and made him swear out loud. When he finished, he smiled at me, "Now you've got it, padre!" and handed me a twenty dollar bill.

It was at St. Mary's that I fell in love with La Raza, that warm, loving, and engaging community of Mexicans with their songs, laughter, faith family ties, and hard work.

With all of these happenings I also fell under the influence of Charlie Philipps during five years of almost daily "briefings" on the state of society, the injustices of corporate power, and the silence of the established church in the face of oppression and injustice.

Leaving St. Mary's in 1955 for two years of graduate school at The Catholic University of America, Washington, D.C., and a Masters Degree in Social Work, I returned to San Francisco to work at Catholic Social Service followed by a five year stay at Hanna Boys Center, Sonoma, working with court referred juvenile delinquent boys until 1962 when the newly formed Diocese of Santa Rosa was founded, and I was appointed as Chancellor of the Diocese.

In Santa Rosa I became reconnected with the Spanish Speaking community. At the time I was the only priest in the diocese who spoke Spanish. I came across the name of a George Ortiz, a social worker in the Sonoma County Department of Social Services who was teaching English classes nearby. We met for lunch where I expressed my desire to get connected to the Mexican community. This encounter led to a life long friendship and community involvement. My love for La Raza continued through my Church and post–Church career through the many Chicano leaders and community activists whom I encountered and worked with: Cesar Chavez and Dolores Huerta of the United Farm Workers, my long time friend Herman Gallegos, Jimmy Delgadillo, Bert Corona, Lee Soto, Al Guzman, Alex Zemeno, Jack Ybarra, Carmen Solis, Margaret Cruz, Sal Alvarez, Candido Morales, and many others.

If I believed in reincarnation, my fantasy would place me somewhere in the Mexican–American War as a member of the St. Patrick's Battalion, that group of Irish immigrants conscripted into the American army, who deserted, joined the Mexican forces, and fought against the Yankees. My desire to connect with La Raza led me to visit Mexico about 20 different times, read Mexican and Chicano history, and learn Mexican songs. As the years progressed, I sensed that Raza people welcomed me into their hearts, not only because of my Roman collar. Years later when my bishop Leo T. Maher was transferred from Santa Rosa to San Diego, California a group of Chicano priests urged Maher to appoint a Chicano priest as an Auxiliary Bishop. However, they informed him that if he could not identify a suitable Chicano, that I could be an acceptable alternative. So I guess my Raza identity had spread all the way to San Diego.

The Mexican American Political Association was one of the early efforts of organizing political power among Mexican American communities in California. I paid for George Ortiz to attend their convention in San Diego. He returned after rubbing shoulders with some of the most influential Mexican American leaders in California., full of fire to organize the Mexican community of Sonoma County. Along with a few others we organized the Latinos Unidos of Sonoma County, developed a scholarship program for graduating high school seniors, organized chapters of Mexican American students in the Sonoma County high schools called MAYO (Mexican American Youth Organization), and finally with Lou Flores and Aurelio Hurtado formed the North Bay Human Development Organization, a multi million dollar human service program of employment, housing, and services for poor people in several counties of Northern California. George and I not only became close friends, but also "compadres" with him as the godfather of our daughter Rebekah.

During this period I had not only my administrative duties in the Bishop's office, but as the only Spanish speaking priest I found myself answering requests for Masses and services in different parts of the diocese. I also became involved in the Latin American Day Conference, an annual gathering of Catholic Spanish speaking groups from Northern California at St. Mary's College, Moraga, California. Attended by lay leaders and religious from various parishes the conference first focused on religious and spiritual activities. However, as the years passed, it soon began to stress community and social problems. One of its highlights was its annual meeting at the Jesuit University of San Francisco in October 1966 with Robert Kennedy as the featured speaker. I still have a letter from him thanking me for inviting him. I framed the letter and have treated it as a first class relic.

The conference led to the establishment of a permanent West Coast Office of the National Bishops' Committee for the Spanish Speaking in Washington, D.C. As Chairman of the conference, I accompanied several laymen to Washington where we advocated for an office which was later approved. Salvador Alvarez from San Jose, California, was hired as the first Director. We received formal approval and backing from the Bishops of Northern California Dioceses. Sal began to advocate for the establishment of local branches in each diocese.

My appointment as a pastor of a newly created parish in West Santa Rosa allowed me to try out some ideas of community building as well as modern church architecture. Bishop Maher at the time suggested that I build a priest's house (rectory) and four classrooms for Sunday liturgies and other functions. I persuaded him on a small neighborhood house as a temporary residence. My architect Tom Fruiht and I had been discussing modern church architecture for years. I was always bothered by traditional church buildings whose use was limited by fixed benches used for only a few hours on Sunday mornings. So Tom and I proposed a multipurpose building with moveable chairs that could be cleared for a large dinner or social function. The altar and sanctuary fixtures were all on casters and could be hidden away behind a large floor to ceiling drape. On one occasion as people were clearing out the chairs to prepare for a dance one of the parishioners remarked, "Hey, Father, look! We can go from a church to a night club in 15 minutes!" We named the parish Resurrection with the notion that we were creating a new community of Christians. A small chapel for week day Mass and meditation along with a parish administrative office completed the structure.

I am very proud that after all these years that the temporary church is still the same and that the priests are living in the same house as members of the neighborhood.

It was also at Resurrection that my life was turned around with the arrival of Sister Kathleen Snyder who came to work as a parish sister. I sensed immediately that we shared common goals about building a parish community, social justice, and working to eradicate social evils. Along with our common spiritual visions, we gradually became personally attracted to each other and fell in love. After Kathleen left her religious community and joined the Peace Corps in Honduras, it took me a few years to decide that I wanted to share my life with her. So I received a formal dispensation from Rome, married, and began a family with our two girls Rebekah and Mary Anne. I was 47 and Kathy 27. Many people over the years have asked me why and how I happened to leave the priesthood, and my reply was that "I had suffered a serious heart attack and had to leave." Our commitment to social justice was passed on to our girls. We all participated in Anti-Vietnam demonstrations, picketed supermarkets for farm workers, and participated in meetings about injustices in Latin America. We lived in the San Francisco Bay Area for a few years, I working in social service positions and Kathy receiving her Masters Degree in Public Health from the University of California, Berkeley.

We discovered the Anderson Valley, Mendocino County, in Northern California where we have resided and raised our family for the past 22 years. Kathy organized a nonprofit housing development organization for farm workers, the Anderson Valley Housing Association, while working as a Health Educator Community-Organizer at our local health center. She later acquired her high school credential and now teaches

Spanish at our small local high school. I directed a Spanish Speaking family center nearby in Ukiah called Nuestra Casa, opened a residential treatment center for teen age drug addicts and alcoholics until it was terminated due to declining referrals, and became active in fund raising for the Health Center and the Housing Association. Both of us remain active with Mexican students who now comprise about sixty percent of our student body. In her role as teacher and consciousness raiser she not only teaches Spanish but also Mexican history and Latin American politics. I also work as a counselor for at risk Mexican boys and their families.

I also initiated the development of a farm workers organization called Sueno Latino which focuses on health and housing issues for farm worker families in the valley. And now our commitments carry over into the next generation as our older daughter Rebekah's long time attraction to Mexican/Latino culture led her to become a bilingual teacher in Windsor, California, where she displays a UFW farm worker flag as well as Chicano movement posters in her classroom. A visiting parent once asked her what was the source of her passion for her students, and she replied, "I was raised by two martyrs." Rebekah's Latino attraction has also resulted in her marriage to a young Mexican from Santa Rosa, California, Jose Rocha, inheriting a large extended family and having a baby named Gerald Cox Rocha. Our younger daughter Mary Anne majored in Women's' Studies, is an active feminist, and is very sensitive to society's uneven playing field.

So my own consciousness raising and social awareness is like a long cord which I can trace back to West Oakland, St. Mary's Church, and the deep influence of Charlie Philipps, as well as a litany of social activists with whom I was privileged to associate, especially Kathleen who still can become enraged at social injustice committed against poor and defenseless people. Her holy anger keeps us both focused on Jesus' message of defending the poor and oppressed. I once met her paternal grandfather in Denver, Colorado, and asked him what she was like as a child. "She was always for the underdog," he replied and so she remains.

One interesting feature of my life as a resigned Catholic priest is that many people whom I have met continue to regard me as a priest. Although I am not functioning as one, people still see me in the role of an ordained cleric. I am called "Padre", "Father", and sometimes "Monsignor", a church title I once possessed. People will also refer to me as one who still has influence "with the Man Upstairs". Although I am no longer able to officiate in the Church, I still maintain a sense of priesthood which now to me means bringing God to people by one's witness and people to Him by living Christ's message through advocating and fighting for the poor and oppressed. Ultimately most Catholics and certainly non-Catholics will welcome a married clergy as do other denominations.

Whenever I pass through Oakland, I drive down to 7th and Jefferson Streets and stop in front of those old shingled buildings, church, rectory, school, and social hall of St. Mary's which have been closed with the exception of Sunday services for a new immigrant community of Vietnamese. The parish plant, once a dusty chocolate brown shingled group of structures, has been renewed by a gleaming white coat and a completely renewed modern sanctuary. The church building once like an old bag lady huddled in a nearby doorway has been made over into an elegant mother who sits there proud of her history since 1852 and remembering her gifts of love, inspiration, and faith which she provided for the thousands of multiracial individuals and families, elderly pensioners, and "down and outers".

It was here that I began a most exciting and enriching chapter of my life which has been expanded into so many thrilling experiences and people. I often look up to Charlie's rectory window and feel that string that not only winds back to him but that also has been unfurled through all of my life experiences. I have been deeply infected by him and blessed.

ISBN 141209557-3

9 781412 095570